For Mr. Keith Bullock on his preaching in the
chapel for the Open Air Mission 5-11-2000

[signature]

The Church That Would Not Die
has been published
in a Limited Edition
of which this is

Number 308

A list of subscribers
is printed at
the back of the book.

THE CHURCH THAT WOULD NOT DIE

FRONT COVER: St Mary's, Castle Street, Reading, 1942. (RCHME)

THE CHURCH THAT WOULD NOT DIE

A New History of St Mary's Castle Street Reading

BY

JOHN DEARING

Preface by Rev Dr D. N. Samuel,
Minister of the Chapel

"It is not orders, or endowments, or liturgies
that will keep a Church alive. Let
free forgiveness through Christ
be faithfully proclaimed in her pulpits, and
the gates of hell shall not prevail against her.
Let it be buried, or kept back, and
her candlestick will soon be taken away."

J. C. Ryle

BARON
MCMXCIII

PUBLISHED BY BARON BIRCH
FOR QUOTES LIMITED IN 1993
AND PRODUCED BY KEY COMPOSITION,
SOUTH MIDLANDS LITHOPLATES, HILLMAN PRINTERS (FROME) LTD,
CHENEY & SONS AND WBC BOOKBINDERS

ISBN 0 86023 526 2

CONTENTS

PREFACE

by Rev Dr D. N. Samuel, Minister of St Mary's, Castle Street

In writing the history of St Mary's Episcopal Chapel, Reading, John Dearing has performed a valuable service, for he reminds us of the nature and place in the Church's history of proprietary chapels. Such places of worship are not now as common as they once were in the 18th and early 19th centuries.

A proprietary chapel, as the name implies, is the property not of the Church of England but of independent trustees who have the right to appoint an incumbent to minister in the chapel. The occasion of St Mary's Chapel being built was the desire on the part of the Trustees and those associated with them to uphold the doctrines of the 39 Articles of Religion of the Church of England and to ensure that they were faithfully preached. That in itself must seem strange, since the Articles were the doctrinal standard of the church to which they already belonged as members of the parish church of St Giles, Reading. Why then, it may be asked, was it necessary to go to the lengths of building a separate chapel in order to ensure that the doctrines of that church to which they belonged were preached? This strange anomaly requires some explanation.

At the Reformation in the 16th century, the Church of England sought to purge itself of many doctrines which had been added to the teaching of Holy Scripture and to return to a clear Biblical position. This is shown quite plainly by the sixth of the 39 Articles, entitled *Of the Sufficiency of the Holy Scriptures for Salvation*. The Bible contains all things that we need to know in order to be saved. Many of the other Articles bring out the great Biblical doctrines of the Fall of man, his inability of himself to turn to God, the need for justification before God by Christ's merits and righteousness through faith alone and the place of good works as the fruits of faith. While such teaching was the dominant note of the Church of England at the Reformation and for some time afterwards, by the early 18th century it was largely neglected and a religion of morality was being preached. The Gospel of grace and faith no longer sounded from her pulpits.

The great Evangelical Awakening of the 18th century, which took place through the preaching of George Whitefield and John Wesley, appeared at first to be something entirely new but, as they themselves pointed out, it was nothing other than the revival of those teachings found in the Bible and in the Articles. These truths had become real in their own experience; they felt their force and power in their lives; they knew what it meant to be sinful, guilty and condemned before God; they knew also the joy and blessedness of pardon, cleansing and justification through faith alone in Jesus Christ. In that age of cold and formal religion they were regarded as enthusiasts and attempts were made to drive them out of the Church of England.

This was what happened in Reading, where the Evangelical Awakening touched the life of the Rector of St Giles, William Bromley Cadogan. Through his preaching many came to a saving faith in Christ and embraced the spiritual doctrines of grace of the 39 Articles. When Cadogan died there was a strong desire for another minister of the Gospel in the same mould. The Bishop and the Patron showed no real understanding of the situation and refused to appoint such a man, with the result that a large part of the congregation left. They went out, like Abraham, 'not knowing whither they went', but like him believing that God had a purpose for them and with the truth of His Word as their guiding star. They were enabled to build a chapel where they could worship God according to the very doctrines of that church they had been compelled temporarily to forsake.

I believe there is in the moving story traced out in this book an important lesson for us today, for we also are now faced with a situation in which there is much defection from sound teaching and in which many are once again strangers to those Bible doctrines of ruin, redemption and regeneration which were at the heart of the Evangelical Awakening. Let us be guided by our forefathers. Let us firmly resolve as they did to put first, before every other consideration, faithfulness to the Word of God and those doctrines of grace which form the everlasting gospel of Our Lord Jesus Christ.

The Parsonage
1 Downshire Square
Reading
Berkshire.

David Samuel

ACKNOWLEDGEMENTS

The author's thanks are due to: the Trustees of St Mary's, Castle Street, and in particular Rev John Reynolds and Dr Roger Beckwith, for their encouragement in the writing of this book; to Dr David Samuel for composing the Preface and checking the final revision of the text; to the following present or past members of the congregation for information provided: the late Miss Phyllis Adams, Mr Tom Barker, Mr Charles Borsley, Mrs Vera Good, Mrs Barbara Hurst, Mrs Ethel O'Neill, Mr Denis Richmond, Mr Gordon Spriggs and Professor Joseph Tinsley; to Dr Derek Scales and to Mr Graham Hutchings for information relating to Rev G. Tubbs and Rev J. Consterdine; to Mr Leslie North for tracking down the story of Jonathan Britain; to Mr John Harber for loan of 'Leakey's Luck', and to the staff of Berkshire County Reference Library, the Berkshire Record Office and the Evangelical Library, London, for their kind and courteous assistance. Thanks are also due to Eddie Stock for photographic services and to Berkshire Libraries, Archives and Tourism and the Royal Commission on Historic Monuments in England for permission to reproduce photographs in their collection.

The cost of publication of this book has been met in part from the legacy left to the Chapel by Mr E. W. 'Bill' Appleby, whose outstanding service to the cause of Christ in Reading will be apparent from the pages that follow.

Key to Caption Credits

RCHME	RCHME Crown Copyright
ES	E. Stock
BLAT	Berkshire, Libraries, Archives & Tourism
CB	C. Birch

THE GREAT AWAKENING 1739-1774

Not long after his conversion John Wesley made a visit to Reading, during which a meeting he was addressing was disrupted by an enraged mob. In his *Journal* for 1 November 1739, he commented: 'Therefore I hope God has a work to do in this place'.

Reading's strategic location between London and Bristol ensured frequent visits from the evangelist; on 10 March 1777 we read a more encouraging report: 'In the evening I preached at Reading. How many years were we beating the air at this town? Stretching out our hands to a people stupid as oxen! But it is not so at present. That generation is passed away, and their children are of a more excellent spirit'. Wesley was able to write so confidently largely because of the events with which the history of St Mary's Chapel begins.

One should not suppose from these comments that Reading in 1739 was in any way exceptional, nor indeed that there lacked pockets of believers among its 8,000 inhabitants. The Congregationalists had been meeting in Broad Street since the Restoration period, while the occasional ministry of Bunyan in Reading is well-known and gave rise to a company of Baptists that assembled behind St Giles' Church before moving in the 1750s to Hosier Lane.

The established Church, however, was in a state of decadence and sterility. The Restoration of the Monarchy of Charles II had secured for it the incomparable liturgical heritage of the *Book of Common Prayer,* but at the same time the enforcement of that liturgy by the Act of Uniformity had drained the Church of much of its life-blood, through the removal of some two thousand ministers of Puritan persuasion. The Broad Street Congregationalists had themselves come into being with the ejection from the Minster Church of St Mary's of Rev Christopher Fowler (1610-76) whose Puritan sympathies earned him the title of 'author of most of the evil in the town' from professing Anglicans, among whom the Vicar of neighbouring St Laurence's took the lead.

The decline of the national Church continued during the early decades of the 18th century. To intolerance and deadness was added apostasy, as the near-agnostic creed of Deism took a grip on theology. Even among the orthodox, religion was a thing of the mind rather than of the heart. During this period, one looks to the dissenters, men such as Watts and Doddridge, for adherence to Gospel truth and a lively faith such as is expressed in their memorable hymns. Even in nonconformity, however, lapses into unitarianism were by no means unknown; in Reading, both the Congregationalists and the Baptists were torn by internal schism which must have blunted their effectiveness. G. R. Balleine characterised this period as 'the Glacial Epoch in our Church History', when the leading preachers of the day boasted that they 'let alone the mysterious points of religion, and preached only plain, practical morality'. Unfortunately, when divorced from the doctrines of Grace, this moral preaching proved singularly ineffective against the widespread immorality of the day.

Such a spiritual drought was a tinder-box for the forest fire of revival that was to sweep across England. Onto the scene came such giants as John Wesley and George Whitefield, with their itinerant ministries, but also numerous others who exercised their ministry within a narrower compass, and whose names are often linked with the scenes of their pastorates: Berridge of Everton, Grimshaw of Haworth and Fletcher of Madeley amont them. Although Wesley's work had led to the formation of a Society in Reading in the late '40s, and one of his lieutenants, John Cennick, was a Reading man, it was largely through this pattern of parochial ministry that the Great Awakening finally reached Reading.

One of the most remarkable participants in the Revival was a lady of the aristocracy, Selina Hastings, Countess of Huntingdon (1707-91), who exercised an influential behind-the-scenes ministry, encouraging and supporting evangelical clergymen, establishing chapels where they were needed, funding the training of men for the ministry, and also evangelising among her own class. One of her protegés was a member of the Talbot family which, in the recent past, had produced a Lord Chancellor and a Bishop of Durham. Rev William Talbot (1717-74) had been converted to a living faith in Christ and (as Leslie Harman rather quaintly puts it) 'gone itinerating under' the Countess's 'orders', while Vicar of Kineton near Banbury. James Hervey of Weston Favell, another noted Evangelical, who met Talbot at this time (1757), described him as a man 'baptized with the Holy Ghost and with fire — fervent in spirit and setting' his face 'as a flint'.

In 1768, Talbot held the living of All Hallows, Upper Thames Street, London; the then Vicar of St Giles-in-Reading, James York, was seeking a prestigious City parish, while Talbot felt that a provincial urban parish of considerable poverty would provide greater scope for his ministry. With the approval of the Lord Chancellor, who had the right of presentation to St Giles, the two arranged an exchange. James York went on from his city base to achieve episcopal glory and longevity as Bishop successively of St Davids, Gloucester and Ely (1781-1808) [i]; William Talbot was destined to live out his briefer span as Vicar of St Giles.

The decline in clothmaking, which had been Reading's major industry, had caused an increase in the number of poor and Talbot devoted much energy to visiting them and those in prison. Above all he preached the Gospel; in the words of one who later inherited his spiritual mantle, Henry Gauntlett, Talbot's preaching 'was accompanied by the sacred energy of the Holy Spirit, and hence it became the power of God to the salvation of many of his hearers'. Another writer characterises Talbot as 'an extraordinary man both for piety and generosity' and reckons that some 200 to 300 souls were converted to Christ during his six years in Reading. At times, it seems that Talbot's generosity was such that he was taken advantage of by the less honest of his flock. He also suffered 'the most unprovoked and cruellest attacks' upon his reputation when his motives in helping to bring to justice the forger, Jonathan Britain, were maliciously misrepresented and he was forced to vindicate himself in the 45-page *Narrative of the Whole of His Proceedings*.

Talbot's wife, Sarah, was a woman of remarkable strength of character who participated to the full in her husband's labours, and both were 'venerated by the congregation and highly esteemed throughout all the town and neighbourhood'.

The close of William Talbot's earthly service to his Lord came suddenly on 2 March 1774. A few days before, he had been about to set out for London, to visit his friend, the Colonial Secretary, Lord Dartmouth, when a request came for him to visit a sick parishioner, suffering from a contagious fever. With his customary sense of duty he attended the sickbed before proceeding on his journey. In London, he was himself struck down by the same sickness and died at the home of another friend, Mr Wilberforce, uncle of the philanthropist.

Wesley was aware of Talbot's work but seems to have both underestimated its results and to have misunderstood the events that followed his death for, on 2 March 1775, he recorded: '. . . met our brethren at Reading. A few were awakened, and perhaps converted here, by the ministry of Mr Talbot; but as he did not take any account of them or join them together, we found no trace of them remaining'. It was certainly neither lack of organisation nor shallowness of calling that caused the initial dispersion of Mr Talbot's hearers.

ABOVE: Reading lay on the road between London and Bristol, ensuring John Wesley's frequent visits; The Reading - London coach provided the main link. BELOW: Churches dominate the 1800s Reading skyline. (CB)

ABOVE: Caversham Park, birthplace of William Cadogan. (BLAT)
BELOW: Reading from Caversham in 1793. (CB)

14

WILLIAM BROMLEY CADOGAN 1774-1797

Above Caversham there stands a mansion which assumed its present shape in 1854 and is now the home of the BBC Monitoring Service. In the second decade of the 18th century, the old manor-house, which had played a part in the Civil War, had been acquired and demolished by General Earl Cadogan. Between 1718 and 1723, he built a grand mansion on the site, the grounds of which were later landscaped by Capability Brown. The first Caversham Park, however, burnt down and the kernel of the present building took its place around 1770.

Around 1784, Charles Sloane Cadogan, 3rd Baron and 1st Earl of the second creation, sold the country seat to a Major Marsack and settled in Suffolk. Ten years earlier, it had been the scene of an unusual event in Reading's ecclesiastical story.

It would appear to have been the Cadogan family's Reading connections that inspired the Lord Chancellor of 1774, Earl Bathurst (1714-94), to offer the Crown living of St Giles-in-Reading, vacated by the death of Talbot, to Charles Sloane Cadogan's second son, William Bromley.

William Bromley Cadogan had been born on 22 January 1751 at the Cadogans' London residence at Bruton Street, Mayfair, [ii] taking his second name from the maiden name of his mother, Frances. She was a pious lady, under whose guidance William was taught the Scriptures. Quite early in his childhood he seems to have felt a strong call to the ministry, which was confirmed when his father took him to see the eminent cleric, Dr John Ewer, Bishop of Llandaff.

In 1769, after schooling at Westminster, Cadogan went up to Christ College, Oxford, where he became noted for his industrious study of the Bible; he painstakingly made an abstract of each of its 66 books for his own use. He was also notorious for his irritable nature; this trait combined with his loathing of Methodism when, in the course of a debate, he threw a salt-cellar into the face of a fellow-student sympathetic to the Evangelical cause.

Tradition has it that Earl Bathurst, passing through Reading on a journey to or from Bath, heard of Talbot's death from the landlord of the Crown Hotel and, aware of his great responsibilities in the matter, 'felt an inclination' there and then to confer the vacant living on Lord Cadogan's grandson; hearing that his Lordship was in residence in Caversham Park, he therefore 'resolved to go himself and make the offer in person'.

It seems the Lord Chancellor was a man not given to ostentation so Lord Cadogan's servants, failing to recognise his status, told him that the master was not at home. Bathurst was obliged to write a note to his fellow peer on a scrap of paper, resting on the kitchen dresser: 'The Lord Chancellor presents compliments to Lord Cadogan, and, understanding he has a grandson in the church, begs his condescending acceptance of the vicarage of St Giles, which he has just heard is become vacant'. Fortunately, the servants realised their mistake and, after profuse apologies, Lord Cadogan gratefully accepted the living on behalf of his grandson.

There was just one slight hitch: William Bromley was still at the University, and not yet ordained. The Lord Chancellor was able to arrange the sequestration of the living until the necessary formalities were completed. A further difficulty after Cadogan's ordination was dealt with by another nice act of expediency. He added to St Giles the living of St Luke's Chelsea, which was in the gift of his family as a result of his grandfather's marriage to a daughter of Sir Hans Sloane. Church regulations stated that plural livings could only be held by Masters of Arts and Cadogan was not yet qualified by age to take his Master's degree at Oxford; however, Archbishop Cornwallis found the young scholar admirably qualified to receive a Lambeth degree and so yet another minor obstacle in the career of Wiliam Bromley Cadogan was overcome.

On Talbot's death, his recently-appointed Curate, John Hallward, had assumed responsibility for the spiritual needs of the parish. Hallward (1749-1826) had been an older contemporary of Cadogan at Oxford and a leader of a small group of evangelical students at the University which had been the birthplace of Methodism. We may suppose that the hapless recipient of the salt-cellar belonged to this group [iii] and that Hallward himself would have been well aware of Cadogan's reputation as a scourge of the Enthusiasts. Likewise, Cadogan would have known his Curate for the kind of man on whom he would have been tempted to inflict assault and battery.

Certainly, the people of St Giles, who had come to saving faith through Talbot's ministry, learnt of Cadogan's appointment with consternation, and could only hope that as a young aristocrat he 'might feel no disposition to do the duties himself' and thus be prepared to employ Hallward as his Curate. Cadogan, however, was no-time-serving pluralist, but a man of strong, if misguided, zeal. On arriving at St Giles, he received a petition signed by many of the parishioners, urging him to retain their beloved Curate; with his customary intemperance he cast it into the fire unread and dismissed Hallward with the rash declaration that he should never preach in his pulpit again — words he would one day gladly eat!

The vicarage fire was on permanent overtime in those days. We learn that John Wesley, hearing of Cadogan's zeal, sent him a collection of his writings, which were also consigned to the flames, Cadogan declaring that he would 'form his opinions from the Bible alone'.

It is scarcely surprising that such goings-on led many of the congregation to seek Gospel-preaching elsewhere. The Baptists of Hosier Lane were experiencing a revival through the ministry of Thomas Davies, who was pastor from 1768 to 1798 and described as 'by far the most lively preacher' in the town. Some found a home there, while others applied to the Countess of Huntingdon, who acquired on their behalf a Chapel that stood in St Mary's, Butts. This building, seating two to three hundred people, is said to have existed since 1734, though its previous history is obscure.

Cadogan made an equally clumsy start to his ministry in Chelsea. Ever zealous, he threw himself into his work by attacking the widespread breaking of the Sabbath among the godless. His attempts to enforce the law were largely ineffective and aroused the fury of tradesmen and labouring classes alike; numbers attending divine service showed no improvement and, much to his chagrin, his plans to enlarge the church were rejected by parishioners.

In this sorry record of so much effort to such little avail, Cadogan reminds us of the young John Wesley, whose inept labours among the colonists of Georgia prior to his conversion bore such meagre fruit. However, as with Wesley, events were moving to the end that Cadogan also might trust in Christ and 'Christ alone for salvation'.

The agent of God's grace was to be that remarkable lady, Mrs William Talbot, a woman 'wise in the things of God', as Cadogan was later to call her, who was to act as Priscilla to her Apollos [Acts 18.26]. Following her bereavement, she had moved to a house in Castle

16

Street. The recently-refurbished No 55, next to the Almshouses, is to this day called Talbot House. There has been fanciful speculation that the handsome sculpture of a dog that surmounts the porch is a representaton of Sarah Talbot's hound — if indeed she possessed one! Those with longer memories attest that the beast in question was originally a fox, with the hound a relatively recent arrival.

Mrs Talbot felt it her duty to assist her late husband's converts in their walk with Christ and, through her contacts with some of his fellow-ministers and her friendship with Lady Huntingdon, was able to arrange meetings in her house at which such prominent Evangelicals as John Newton, William Romaine and Henry Venn expounded the Gospel. Rowland Hill (1744-1833), who had led a similar movement at Cambridge University to that which Cadogan encountered at Oxford, and was on intimate terms with John Hallward, was another whose association with Reading dates from then.

Sarah Talbot, however, was not one to rest content with a situation in which Anglican Evangelicals had no permanent home in Reading. She perceived that quality in Cadogan that others had missed, which might be turned to the service of the Gospel. Prayers for him were offered at the house meetings and Sarah herself engaged him in correspondence with an importunity that initially incurred his deep resentment but eventually won his heart. In his funeral sermon for Mrs Talbot (November 1785) Cadogan warmly acknowledged that her letters and example had been the 'principal means of leading him to the saving knowledge of Christ'. He regarded her 'not only as the best friend I ever had in my life, but as a mother to me in love'.

His conversion took place about two years after his arrival in Reading, but even then it was a further two years before he felt able to make a full public declaration of his change of heart — such was the opprobrium in which 'enthusiasm' was held in the circles frequented by his family.

The period of Cadogan's most effective ministry in Reading dates, therefore, from 1780, and it was in September that he attempted to 'make reparation' for a 'former injury' by inviting John Hallward to resume his curacy. Hallward could not accept, as he had recently been appointed to a living elsewhere, but instead he came to Reading on an extended visit, renewing old friendships and seeking to encourage Cadogan in his new-found resolution.

Hallward's unavailability led to the arrival of another character who came to play a signficant role. John Eyre (1754-1803) of Bodmin in Cornwall was Cadogan's Curate from 1781-5. He had studied at Lady Huntingdon's training college at Trevecca in Wales and had subsequently officiated at several of her chapels, including one at Mulberry Gardens, London. He later decided to enter regular Anglican orders and, after studies at Emmanuel College, Cambridge, was ordained in 1779. He came to Reading after two brief curacies, at Weston and at Lewes, where Richard Cecil, a friend and future biographer of Cadogan, was the incumbent. As Cadogan came increasingly to make Reading the chief focus of his ministry, much of John Eyre's time was spent in Chelsea but this did not prevent him from courting and in 1785 marrying a Reading girl named Mary Keene.

Shortly after his marriage, Eyre was appointed Minister of a proprietary chapel at Homerton, set up by a Mr Ram. Homerton was then a growing and impoverished district of East London where the church was largely conspicuous by its absence. Eyre remained at Ram's Chapel to the end of his earthly labours, but was also involved in several enterprises that won him a wider reputation. In 1793, he established the *Evangelical Magazine,* with a view to harnessing the growing power of the press to the cause of Christ. In 1794, he was one of a small group of ministers, both Anglicans and dissenters, who met to found what would become known as the London Missionary Society. Eyre was a founding Director; the Society helped to pioneer overseas missions from Great Britain; he also formed a society to encourage home evangelism in the southern counties.

17

William Cadogan had now begun to preach the Gospel with great power; those who had deserted to the Countess's chapel in the Butts flocked back to St Giles, and the pragmatic Countess duly closed her chapel down. In spite of his learning and pedigree, Cadogan possessed the rare gift of communicating great truths simply so that the most illiterate members of the congregation were able to comprehend them. The titles of some of his sermons bound up with Cecil's *Memoir* illustrate this direct approach: 'The Power of Faith', 'The Love of Christ', 'The Friendship of God'. Before preaching, he would always pray, 'Lord, send us not empty away', and we may readily believe that his hearers were always filled with good spiritual meat. He saw it as his duty to exalt the crucified Christ, quoting the words of the Saviour in John 12: 'I, if I be lifted up, will draw all men unto me'.

Like Talbot, he was diligent in visiting the poor and sick and was generous in offering practical help. To the better off, he would say, 'If you are well, you must not expect me often; if you are sick, I shall never fail to visit you constantly'. Cecil records that during the winter the 'poor of the parish had meat and broth every day', with the result that the Vicarage budget had to allow for 30 lbs of beef per week! Cadogan would also help out fellow-clergymen in financial straits. He proved himself a devoted husband, too, after his marriage in 1782 to the widow of a Captain Bradshaw.

Cadogan's high connections could easily have gained him preferment but he declined the offer of a chaplaincy to the Lord Lieutenant of Ireland, who had undertaken to confer on him the first Irish bishopric that fell vacant.

Although Cadogan became a humbler man after his conversion, and his tantrums were correspondingly rarer, he retained his strength of personality. In the pulpit, his manner was forcible and his delivery a little rough. He was certainly not afraid of pointing out a few home truths, as in his Address to his Parishioners in 1785: 'It is impossible to have been ten years your Minister, and not to have observed the general neglect of those holy things, in which I am sent to minister among you; a neglect which I cannot but observe with concern, not as it is insulting to myself, but as it is dishonouring to God, and consequently bringing upon yourselves swift destruction: for God's rate of proceeding is invariable, "them that honour me I will honour, and they that despise me, shall be lightly esteemed".'

Cadogan strengthened the faith of two men who were to become important Evangelical leaders. Charles Simeon (1759-1836), after his conversion at Cambridge, sought out both Cadogan and Mrs Talbot, during visits to his family in Reading — to such evident good effect that at first his father forbade him to continue to fraternise with these troublesome folk. Happily, old Mr Simeon became reconciled to his son and secured for him the incumbency of Holy Trinity, Cambridge, where he laboured over fifty years and influenced a generation of younger men.

William Marsh (1775-1864) began to attend St Giles after a conversion experience in 1793 and was, in Cadogan's words 'pleased to stile' himself 'my son in the faith'. Marsh boosted the evangelical cause in Reading during his curacy of St Laurence's and later had a distinguished ministry in Birmingham, Leamington Spa and Beckenham. He once said of Cadogan: 'He showed me that' the Bible 'was the Word of God' and 'the only book in the World which could teach the way of salvation'.

Cadogan offered to enlarge St Giles at his own expense but, as with his earlier proposals for St Luke's, these were turned down by the congregation, not through any animosity but because they were afraid that after his death the extra room might not be needed! This proved all too justified. Instead, Cadogan had to be content with installing the galleries which were such a bugbear to the ritualists who gained control of St Giles in the mid-19th century.

Although he came of a largely long-lived family, Cadogan was called to rest at the early age of 46, on 18 January 1797, as a result of an inflammation of the bowels. He was buried eight days later in St Giles, where a tablet celebrating him — and the Saviour he sought to exalt — was erected in the north aisle. Though his conversion had met with the disapproval of some of the important citizens of the town, he received a tribute at the Assize Sermon, preached in St Laurence's on 8 March. The preacher was the famous pioneer of education in Reading, Dr Valpy: 'Raised as he was by birth and connections to claim the highest honours in the Church, he preferred the useful task of preaching the Gospel to the poor to the splendid scenes of public life ... In all things he shewed himself a pattern of good works; and he, who was of a contrary part, had no evil thing to say of him'.

Let the last word on Wiliam Bromley Cadogan come from one who could be described as his disciple, and who was called upon to preach his funeral sermon. In trying to bring comfort to an apprehensive congregation, Charles Simeon used words from the 13th chapter of Hebrews that Cadogan himself had chosen at the church's motto for the year 1797: 'Go on ... strong in the grace that is in Christ Jesus; and doubt not, but that you shall find the grace of Christ as sufficient for you, as it has been for him; and that what Christ has been to others in former ages, He will be to you, *the same yesterday, today and for ever*'. It was to prove a truly prophetic word, however grim the outlook.

LEFT: St Giles, Reading, prior to restoration in 1872. (BLAT) RIGHT: Memorial to William Bromley Cadogan in St Giles, Reading. (ES)

ABOVE: One of the Three Ancient Churches of Reading, St Laurence's,
in 1802. BELOW: Albion Place, Reading, designed by Richard Billing II.
(BLAT)

A NEW SPECIES OF DISSENTERS 1797-1798

In seeking a successor to Cadogan, the people of St Giles naturally wanted to ensure that the Gospel would still be preached and obtained the support of 'a person of high respectability' to undertake the necessary lobbying with the Lord Chancellor. This person was, however, pipped at the post by another eminent local gentleman, who put forward a Mr Allcock. The *Reading Mercury* of 4 February announced confidently that it ws 'informed that the Rev Mr Allcock is to succeed to the Vicarage of St Giles'.

Mr Allcock was understood to be a man of Evangelical convictions and no doubt the congregation heaved sighs of relief at this turn of events. In the meantime, Simeon's funeral sermon was printed and passed into its second edition within a week — a sure sign of intense public interest in the future ministry at St Giles.

Then came the bombshell — Mr Allcock declined the offer on the grounds that he was unable 'to fill with advantage a pulpit' that had been 'occupied . . . by so great a man as Mr Cadogan'. His patron was evidently not a man to make great distinction between different schools of religion, for 'unmoved by entreaties to consult the general wishes of the people', he 'secured the gift for another' who was as far from Cadogan and his disciples in matters of faith as chalk from cheese.

Rev Joseph Eyre (1752-1815) — not to be confused with his very different namesake, John — was Vicar of Ambrosden near Bicester and also chaplain to the Earl of Elgin (of Marbles fame [iv]), a connection which may have helped to confirm his suitability in the eyes of Lord Chancellor Loughborough. Eyre's appointment was announced in the *Mercury* on 18 February — just a month after his predecessor's passing. We are sometimes inclined to marvel at the lengthy interregna that occur in our own day — in 1797, it was more a case of 'appoint in haste, repent at leisure!'.

At first the parishioners were inclined to take a wait-and-see line with Mr Eyre, perhaps remembering that, if it had not been for the patience of one of their number, they might never have enjoyed the ministry of their beloved William Cadogan; certainly there was no resumption of the petitioning that had greeted and irritated *him*. Nevertheless, a growing sense of disquiet led one member to correspond with the Independent pastor of Maidenhead, John Cooke (1760-1828), whose sage advice is contained in *Five Letters to a Friend*. Cooke, who might have been expected to encourage a flight to the citadels of dissent, rather counselled his young friend to avoid making hasty decisions, but at the end of the day, 'if the gospel removes from St Giles's to St Mary's or any other church in Reading, follow it, and leave St Giles' to the 'owls and dragons'.

Some parishioners may have been attracted by an open offer to the 'sacramental table' of the Broad Street congregation but those who remained faithful to St Giles attempted to 'obtain the nomination of a curate or lecturer' to officiate at their own expense in one of the three ancient churches of Reading, or alternatively to open up a Proprietary Chapel.

The Vicars of St Mary's, St Laurence's and (hardly surprisingly) St Giles' all refused to countenance either of these proposals and it must have been with a sense of frustration and deep disappointment that the congregation finally decided to go it alone, leaving St Giles to those owls and dragons. As a temporary measure they rented the Countess of Huntingdon's disused chapel in the Butts from a Mr Litherland for £44 14s, and services began 'according to the established mode of worship' on Sunday 14 January 1798. Two friends of Reading, Rowland Hill and John Eyre, preached at the morning and afternoon services. A minister was appointed, Rev William Green, one of the Trevecca students whose disbarment from episcopal ordination had led to the secession of the Countess of Huntingdon's Connexion in 1783. His salary was fixed at £130 a year.

Meanwhile, a considerable honour was awaiting Joseph Eyre. As, so to speak, 'the new boy', he was invited to preach a sermon at St Mary's Church on 30 July during the Triennial Visitation of the Bishop of Salisbury. Recent events being much on his mind, he chose the occasion to damn his predecessor with faint praise and castigate the 'Schismatics and Sectaries' that had deserted the pews of St Giles'.

Published as *A Dispassionate Enquiry into the Probable Causes and Consequences of Enthusiasm*, with the text from Romans 10, 'They have a zeal of God, but not according to Knowledge', the sermon was a poorly-argued attack on central evangelical doctrines, including election and predestination, the New Birth and the indwelling of the Holy Spirit. 'Of this very masterly discourse, we cannot view the charge of flattery, when we assert that it was candid, eloquent and learned'. No doubt this fulsome praise earned the Editor of the *Reading Mercury* (who also urged that the sermon should be published forthwith) Mr Eyre's life-long friendship. However, to one evangelical observer, effectively accusing Eyre of serious heresy, it was 'a miserable farrago of Pelagian and Socinian errors, undisguised by ingenuity and unembellished by elocution'.

Joseph Eyre also received mockery from the Evangelical camp through his repeated use of the phrase 'we all of us' to describe his fellow-clergy of the rational school. If the *Mercury* writer is to be believed, the sermon won 'the peculiar approbation' of both the Bishop of Salisbury and the clergy on parade. Certainly Bishop John Douglas (1721-1807), though a noted apologist who defended the authenticity of the biblical miracles against the philosopher, David Hume, was a sceptical Scot when it came to contemporary manifestations. He particularly enjoyed exposing spiritual phenomena such as the Cock Lane Ghost (an enterprise in which he enjoyed Dr Johnson's assistance) and may well have been sufficiently distrustful of Enthusiasm to have forgiven Eyre his inelegancies of expression and to have nodded his head as he rebuked the 'youthful levities and excesses' of his wayward flock.

Eyre's arguments were vigorously attacked in several pamphlets. One of these, by a well-read layman and founder-member of our chapel, Mr Thomas Willats of Kidmore End, was entitled *An Apology for the Church of Christ*. Published in November 1798, it inspired a counterblast from the Chaplain to the new Gaol, Rev Dr Edward Barry (1759-1822), a man whose rational disposition did not prevent him from acting also as Chaplain to the Freemasons. His contribution was called *The Friendly Call of Truth and Reason to a new Species of Dissenters*. Barry, who himself lived in Castle Street, is now better remembered for his worthy efforts to control the spread of rabies.

If there were any waverers remaining among Mr Cadogan's responsive hearers, the Visitation Service must have been the last straw. In any case, work was already in hand to build the new Chapel which is the subject of this history. Its forerunner in the Butts could seat five hundred at a tight squeeze, but this was not enough to accommodate that tithe of Reading's poopulation that wanted both Gospel preaching and Prayer Book worship. By God's providence, a suitable Town Centre location had recently become available.

The old County Gaol and Debtors' Prison in Castle Street had become redundant on the opening in 1794 of a new place of incarceration on the present site in the Forbury. Indentures drawn up during meetings of the Quarter Sessions held at Newbury on 17/18 April 1798, between the Justices of Peace for the County of Berkshire and what was to become the Committee of Management (antecedents of the present Trustees) of the Castle Street Chapel, conveyed the old gaol to Peter French and others. They made a down-payment of one guinea and agreed to pay the remaining £873 19s of the purchase price within one year.

The site itself has been the subject of much speculation by historians of both the sensationalist and scientific schools. No evidence has been found to substantiate the story that Reading's Castle — if, indeed, it ever had one — stood here. The suggestion that there was a house of Franciscans — possibly an offshoot of those who worshipped at what is now Greyfriars Church — is rather better-founded. The Tudor topographer, John Leland, writing in the 1540s, refers to 'a late fayre house of the Grey Freres in Castle Strete', the cells of which became available for less religious uses on the dissolution of the monasteries. The chapel of this friary may have continued to be used for religious worship by the prisoners, if Doran, writing in 1835, is to be believed; he tells us that during the demolition of the gaol 'a small lancet window was discovered next to the street; and a round arch on the east side which was supposed to be the entrance to a chapel for the use of the prisoners' and was 'thought to be of some antiquity'.

Legend has it that John Bunyan was for a time imprisoned in this gaol for his illegal preaching. The truth of this may never be known; for certain the Quaker grandparents of the Reading-born hymn-writer, John Cennick, were incarcerated here on account of their faith, earning their living by making and selling lace. To another Reading poet, James Merrick (1720-69), are attributed lines said to have been inscribed over the gate to excite pity for the poor debtors within — and perhaps to 'discourage the others':

'O ye whose hours exempt from sorrow flow,
Behold the seat of pain, of want and woe,
Think while your hands the entreated alms extend,
That what to us you give to God you lend.'

A description from one of the reports of the prison reformer, John Howard, quoted by Peter Southerton in *The Story of a Prison,* offers a rather uninviting picture of prison life in the 18th century:

'Debtors and felons have their courts separated by iron rails. The former have a kitchen; and for the Master's side many rooms but no free yard . . . The night room for men is a huge dungeon down four steps; the prisoners broke out lately. A separate night-room for women. The turnkey now has a lodging-room over the felons' dungeon, with an alarm-bell so that an escape will be more difficult.'

When Howard made his inspection in 1779, the prison population consisted of nine felons, nine debtors and no fewer than nine unfortunates who were awaiting escort to Spithead after being press-ganged into His Majesty's Navy.

The architect chosen for the new chapel was Richard Billing (1747-1826). No great feats were expected of him, the original building consisting of a simple rectangular preaching box, to which the chancel, porch and turret were added in Victorian times. It seems, however, to have been the only building of any distinction designed by Billing senior, who made up for his own modest output by spawning a whole family of architects.

His son, Richard Billing II (1785-1853), was Surveyor to the Corporation and built some of the splendid Regency buildings that still grace Reading's streets, including Eldon Square and the recently refurbished Albion Place; he was also an active member of the Castle Street Chapel. His son, John (1816-63) was responsible for the West Front of Holy Trinity, the original St John's Church and for several public buildings in the town; he also had a London practice, where Philip Webb was for a while one of his pupils. John's younger brother, Arthur, designed St John the Baptist Church at Kidmore End.

The new chapel was completed within a few months at a cost of just over £2,000. Almost three-quarters of the cost was raised through public subscription, with the difference made up by interest-free loans. Its opening must have been awaited with eager anticipation, not least by that half of the potential congregation unable to obtain access to the Butts Chapel. At last, on 10 December, the *Reading Mercury* was able to announce that 'Sunday the 16th inst was the day fixed for the opening of the New Chapel in the town'. At this point the old Butts Chapel seems finally to have closed its doors; from the mid-19th century it was used by Holmes the furnishers until its demolition in the 1930s for road widening.

In the wider world, the throne was occupied by George III, enjoying a respite from his periodic bouts of insanity. His chief minister, William Pitt, was in the 15th year of his long ministry. The Attorney-General was the hard-liner, John Scott, and the Speaker of the House of Commons, Henry Addington — men who, as Lords Eldon and Sidmouth, were later to lend their names to streets in Reading.

England was at war with the France of Napoleon Bonaparte. The Parliament that assembled on 20 November had congratulated Horatio Nelson, newly created Baron Nelson of the Nile, on the 'great and brilliant victory' that had prevented the French from gaining control of Egypt.

Patriotic fervour was rife, with Nelson's victory boosting those 'demonstrations of zeal and spirit among the ranks of all my subjects' that had led earlier in the year to the establishment of local Volunteer Corps and had even deflected the people of Reading from their religious preoccupations — some of those who helped to pay for the Castle Street Chapel also appear on the lists of those who contributed to the 'Voluntary Subscription for the Defence of the State' during the summer's invasion scare.

As a result of the war, public expenditure had risen from £16 million in 1793 to £29 million. The Government came to realise it could not rely for ever on the voluntary contributions of men of goodwill and on 3 December Parliament accepted the Prime Minister's proposed Income Tax, designed to bring in extra revenue of £10 milllion on a standard rate of 10%. One opponent described the tax as 'indiscriminate rapine' — perhaps there were even some in that first Castle Street congregation who suffered from sore pockets!

In the world of the arts Haydn's oratorio, *The Creation*, was first performed. As there is evidence that two of the artists who took part in the first Reading performance in 1819 had connections with the Castle Street Chapel, it was thus doubly appropriate that it was chosen to be performed during the festival that marked the Chapel's 175th anniversary in 1973.

Former Countess of Huntingdon Chapel in St Mary's Butts, ABOVE: in use as Holmes Furniture Store and BELOW: during demolition in 1930s. (BLAT)

1798. An Account of subscriptions received for building a Chapel &c.

Subscriptions			1st Instalment			2d Do.		
100	Mr Ring	Market Place	50			50		
100	Mr Peter French	Do	50			50		
50	Jno C. Marsh	Fryan Street	25			25		
50	Wm Wood Esqr	Caversham	25			25		
50	Mr May	Englefield	25			25		
50	Mr Jno Tanner	Castle St	25			25		
50	Mr Thos Tanner	Do	25			25		
30	Miss Hanson	Mill Lane	15			15		
30	Mr Lawrence	Market Place	15			15		
30	Messrs Rugmans	Broad Street	15			15		
25	Mr Holloway	Crown Lane	12	10		12	10	
25	Mr Herbert	Castle Street	12	10		12	10	
25	Mr Swallow	Broad St	12	10		12	10	
25	A friend by Do	Mr Billing	12	10		12	10	
22 10	Mr Jos Davis	Market Place	11	5		11	5	
20	Mrs Hanson	Mill Lane	10			10		
20	Mrs Littleworth	Abby House	10			10		
20	Mr Johnson	Southampton St	10			10		
20	Mr Baylis	Do	10			10		
20	Mr C. Truss	Kew	10			10		
20	Mr Richards	West St	10			10		
20	Mr Jno Young	Church St	10			10		
18	Mr Howard	Fryar St	9			9		
15	Mr Legg	Butts	7	10		7	10	
20	Mr Cocky	Castle St	10			10	0	

Extract from Account Book listing subscriptions for building the chapel,
1798. Thomas Ring and Peter French head the page.

FIRST YEARS OF THE NEW CHAPEL 1798-1807

When the new chapel was finally opened, the occasion merited a fulsome report in the January 1799 edition of the *Evangelical Magazine:*
'The new chapel erected at Reading, by the voluntary contribution of the late Mr Cadogan's congregation was opened on Sunday, December 16th. Mr Eyre, of Hackney, preached in the morning, Mr Green, minister of the chapel in the afternoon, and the Rev Rowland Hill in the evening. The collections on this occasion, amounted to £128 which, with the previous subscription of £1650 [v] and some other promised donations, will nearly defray the whole expense of this neat, spacious and commodious building. Notwithstanding the place is calculated to seat conveniently 1000 persons, with considerable spaces in the aisles and under the galleries, it was crowded with serious and attentive hearers, who appeared to receive the word of God with much affection. The sight was truly encouraging, and brought to recollection the words of our Lord, "The fields are white already unto harvest".'

Though the 1790s saw the beginnings — with such ventures and the London Missionary Society — of active cooperation between Evangelicals in the Independent churches and those of the Establishment, and Cadogan, for instance, had quickly established a friendship with the new Minister of Broad Street, Archibald Douglas, it was still a brave thing for a group of Anglicans to turn themselves into 'a new species of dissenters', to use Edward Barry's somewhat Darwinian terminology. What manner of men, therefore, were these courageous 'partial conformists', who built our Chapel?

The five leading lights named in the indentures of 17 and 18 April were: Peter William French, chemist and druggist; Thomas Ring, surgeon; Jonathan Tanner, common brewer; and Thomas Tanner, linen and woollen draper — all these of Reading; and James May, yeoman, of Englefield. The first three of these are of particular interest for their part in the wider history of Reading, as well as that of the Castle Street Chapel.

Dr Thomas Ring (1761-1840), a native of Basingstoke, practised medicine in the Market Place, in partnership with a Dr Bulley. He was later physician to the Duke of Wellington, and Chairman of the Reading Dispensary Committee. In this latter office, he played a leading role in the foundation of the Royal Berkshire Hospital, which was opened the year before his death. A memorial to Dr Ring in the North Chapel of St Laurence's Church refers to him as a founder and supporter of 'St Mary's Chapel in this town' and characterises him as 'a fearless professor of the faith of Christ crucified'.

Mr Peter French also practised his apothecary arts in the Market Place, and indeed he and Dr Ring were close friends. Castle Street was not the only church building project on which these two energetic men were engaged in 1798. It was in that same year Peter French, supported by Dr Ring, founded a small chapel at Peppard at his own expense, contributing £50 per annum to its upkeep. This chapel can be regarded as the prototype of the network of missionary out-stations later established in the villages around Reading, most of which were 'in a fearful state of heathenism and immorality'.

27

Peter French's son, also called Peter (1800-78), married a daughter of Dr Valpy, of whom he had been a pupil, entered the Anglican ministry, and was for 47 years Vicar of Burton-on-Trent. He died in Reading, having received his last communion at St Laurence's Church. His son, Thomas Valpy French (1825-91), was educated in Reading and may as a boy have worshipped with his grandfather. St Mary's, Castle Street, can therefore claim him as its first Bishop for, after many years in the service of the Church Missionary Society (CMS) in India, he ultimately became (1877-87) the first Bishop of Lahore. During one of his home spells he was curate to William Marsh at Beddington in Surrey; in his episcopal role, he was a speaker at the Reading Church Congress of 1883.

That eminently readable 19th century raconteur, William Darter, has much to say about Jonathan Tanner, brewer. Apart from describing a serious fire at his Castle Brewery in Bridge Street in 1811, he records that Mr Tanner also owned King's Meadow, the grass from which doubtless made hay for his dray-horses. The Thames there was popular as a bathing-place for Reading youth, who liked nothing better than playing in the hay after taking their dip. The warfare between Mr Tanner and these young rascals, among whom, one suspects, Darter himself was numbered, reached such a climax that in desperation he resorted to filling up the water with broken bottles to discourage the boys, so that 'ever afterwards this gentleman had the questionable honour of being dubbed Mr Bottle Tanner'. In spite of his rather undignified episode, Mr Tanner was a man of imposing appearance, who wore a powdered wig with a pigtail at a time when this style was fast going out of fashion, and hessian boots. An early entry in the Chapel accounts includes £32 6s paid to Mr Tanner for wine.

The Castle Brewery was later taken over by Messrs Blandy and Hawkins, the latter also a Castle Street Trustee, ultimately becoming part of the Simonds empire. In spite of the abstentionist stance of many clergy, the brewing trade was often associated with evangelical churches. The Hewetts and Dymore Browns were other Reading brewers who became prominent supporters of St Mary's, Castle Street during the 19th century.

Other prominent tradesmen who subscribed to the building of the new Chapel included Mr Quelch, the milliner, Mr Swallow, the nurseryman, Mr Joseph Young, bacon-merchant and first Treasurer, and two other drapers in addition to Thomas Tanner, Messrs Lawrance and Richards.

William Green took up residence at the Chapel House next to the new chapel. This building, which dates from 1751 and is now given over to a variety of commercial purposes including a Post Office, was rented from Richard Billing at £25 pa. Green seems to have given satisfaction, for his salary was increased to £150 pa in 1799, though at the same time he had to pay the rent of the house.

He quickly established friendly relations with fellow Evangelical minsters for, on 16 April 1799, he participated in a regional conference — rather an innovation in those days of doing rather than talking — held at Broad Street, at which John Cooke of Maidenhead was a speaker and in which ministers from as far afield as Basingstoke, Abingdon and Staines took part. Later that year, on Whitsunday, he was among several invited by the Minister of the Peppard Chapel, Joseph Walker (1775-1828), to preach to the young people attending, 'the annual revel' held in the village. His text was John 4.10, 'He would give thee living water'.

The preaching at Peppard was evidently much blessed and afterwards 'a dinner was given to the poor and to the children of the Sunday School; and it gave much pleasure to see many young people prefer the house of God to the revel, which was very thinly attended'. Thereafter, the Whitsun mission to Peppard became an annual event and in later years James Sherman was one of the preachers.

Sadly, William Green was stricken with ill-health during the following twelve months and in the autumn of 1800 felt no longer fit enough to continue his ministry. The Committee was 'unwilling to dismiss him without affording him the means of support' and made him an ex-gratia payment of £150 (a year's salary) which was funded by a second round of interest-free loans. Green did not long survive his removal to London, but his widow was able to use the advance to set up a successful millinery concern in Bond Street. Her son, another William, was to become, in Dr Ring's words, 'a Minister in our excellent Established Church'.

The Chapel was without a resident Minister for the next two years, though a Rev Mr Thorn made frequent appearances in the pulpit, usually at a guinea a time, with occasional support from a Mr Madan and a Rev Mr Toun. The Chapel House was rented out to Mr Joseph Rugman, a member of the congregation. In October 1802, a Mr Bickerdike was engaged at £20 per quarter — rather a drop on William Green's salary, but at the same time he was responsible for his own domestic arrangements. Though he remained in office until the summer of 1805, he is a totally obscure figure — so much so that some historians have managed to lose sight of him altogether! Even so, he did not entirely disappear from the scene, returning to preach for a limited period in 1809.

The same obscurity does not rest on his successor who, though the father of a famous son, was a distinguished preacher and Bible scholar in his own right — and one of a select band of Castle Street ministers to appear, along with Cadogan and John Eyre, in the *Dictionary of National Biography,* the others being James Sherman and Harrington Lees.

Henry Gauntlett (1761-1833) was a Wiltshireman who, after his ordination in 1786, took the curacies of two village parishes near his home town of Lavington. He later became associated with the pioneer of religious education, Hannah More, to whom he provided material about rustic life in Wiltshire which was embodied in the best-known of her forbiddingly entitled *Repository Tracts, The Shepherd of Salisbury Plain.* In 1800, after his marriage to a Vicar's daughter, Arabella Davies, he moved to Botley, near Southampton, and thence in 1804 to Wellington in Shropshire.

About this time, Gauntlett experienced doubts over the Church's doctrine of Baptismal Regeneration. As a result, when alerted to the vacancy that had arisen in Reading, he was attracted by the 'partial conformity' of the Castle Street situation. It was Rowland Hill's elder brother, Sir Richard Hill (1732-1808), who wrote to Gauntlett: 'I am informed by Mrs Rowland Hill that she thinks a minister is wanted at Reading, in Berkshire, for a large Chapel there, instituted exactly upon the same plan as that of my brother's; and if the minister chooses to take a few pupils, there is no doubt but he might have some there. The congregation consists of the late Mr Cadogan's hearers, and they are for the most part zealous for the Church; and therefore, if they cannot hear the Gospel in it, are resolved to keep as near it as they can'.

Gauntlett's ministry commenced in August 1805 and lasted till October 1807, when he seems to have satisfied himself of the orthodoxy of the Thirty Nine Articles in regard to baptismal doctrine sufficiently to accept the livings of Nettlebed and Pishill. These had been previously held by William Marsh from 1801-4, concurrently with his curacy of St Laurence's.

During his time at Castle Street, Gauntlett produced a *Selection of Psalms and Hymns suited to Public and Family Worship'.* Copies were sold to the poor at a subsidised price of 1s 6d — a 6d discount on the marked price.

After his departure, Gauntlett remained a friend of the Castle Street congregation and in 1810 came to their defence with his *Letters to the Stranger in Reading by Detector.* The Stranger himself was John Man, a noted historian of Reading, but also a sceptic who poured

St Mary's Church Castle Street

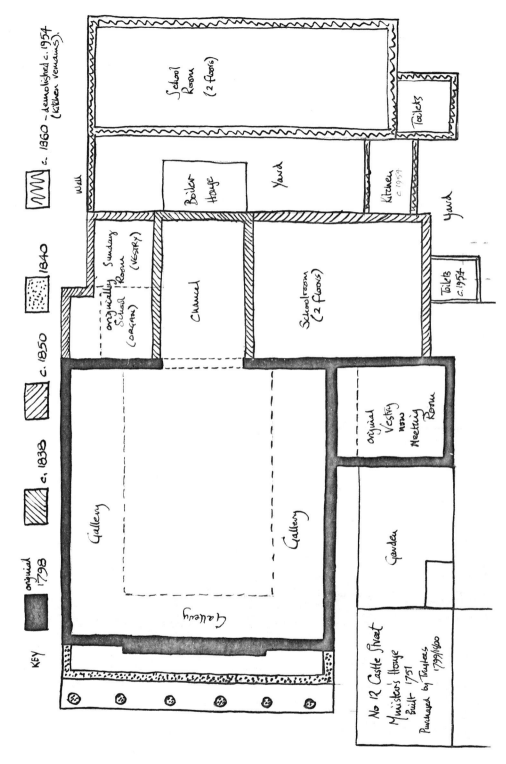

KEY

original 1798

c. 1798

c. 1838

c. 1850

1840

c. 1860 – demolished c. 1954 (kitchen remains).

Wall

School Room (2 floors)

Toilets

Boiler House

Yard

Kitchen c. 1954

Yard

originally Sunday School Room (VESTRY) (ORGAN)

Chancel

Schoolroom (2 floors)

Toilets c. 1954

Gallery

Gallery

Gallery

original Vestry now Meeting Room

Garden

No 12 Castle Street Minister's House Built 1751 Purchased by Trustees 1799/1800

Sketch plan of St Mary's, Castle Street, indicating periods of construction.

scorn on the religious disposition of the town's inhabitants, observing disparagingly that in Reading 'the book most read is the Bible'. Gauntlett saw it otherwise: 'This assertion, Sir, is the highest compliment you can possibly pay to the inhabitants of Reading. If this be a fact, as I am inclined to hope it may, the people of this town . . . afford a most honourable and decisive criterion of the excellence of their taste, as well as the sincerity of their piety'.

The fourth letter includes an important description of the type of worship found in Castle Street in these early years:

'There is another class of Methodists, Calvanistic in their doctrinal sentiments, which was formed and patronised by the late and excellent Lady Huntingdon. These use the Liturgy of the Established Church and in imitation of the national clergy, wear the surplice, gown and band; but I believe their ministers are always previously ordained, and that by far the greater part of them have studied at their college'.

Gauntlett is, however, at pains to distinguish between the Countess's Connexion proper, which had formally seceded from the Church of England, and the Castle Street congregation, which retained its essential allegiance to the Establishment.

In 1811 Gauntlett took on the curacy of Olney, Bucks, the scene of John Newton's labours, where he remained till his death, having succeeded to the living in 1815. During this final period, he published an exposition of Revelation, in which he argued against those who expected Christ to reign on earth in person during the Millenium. A keen interest in the prophecies of the Second Coming will be found among later Castle Street incumbents.

Just before the family's arrival in Reading, Arabella Gauntlett had given birth to a son. Henry John Gauntlett (1805-76) was a musical prodigy who retired as orgaist of his father's church at the grand old age of 19! He is now best known for his splendid hmn tunes including Irby ('Once in Royal David's City'), St Albinus ('Jesus Lives') St Fulbert ('Ye Choirs of New Jerusalem') and University College ('Oft in danger, oft in woe'). As a musician, he worked with the organ-builder, Hill, to improve the range and efficiency of English church organs and was chosen by Mendelssohn to play the organ part in the first production of *Elijah* in 1846. It was thus fitting that this oratorio should also have been performed, during the Chapel's 175th anniversary celebrations.

The manse at Peppard with chapel adjoining, c1900.

The 1800s brought crisis to St Mary's but the decade to 1820 was less
eventful. Business as usual in the 1830s, Market Place, Reading. (CB)

TIMES OF CRISIS 1808-1820

The departure of Henry Gauntlett was followed by a double crisis in the history of the Castle Street Chapel, the first of many that have beset it over the years. The Committee of Management was still dominated by that group of staunch Anglicans who had taken the brave step towards 'partial conformity' ten years previously. In the meantime, an alternative outlet for Anglican Evangelicals had opened up with the ministry of William Marsh at St Laurence's, while a number of folk less sympathetic to the Establishment had been attracted into membership of Castle Street. These began to rebel against the use of the Prayer Book, and particularly the service of the Lord's Supper, but the Committee adamantly resisted any changes. So solidly loyal were they to the Church of their upbringing that their children were taken to one or other of the three parish churches to be baptised and no font was to be found in the Chapel itself.

Eventually, the dissidents broke away and, along with a few Hosier Lane Baptists and Broad Street Independents with equally itchy feet, reopened a chapel in Minster Street that had previously been used by Presbyterians. The Salem Chapel, with its pastor, Thomas Wood (1778-1846) and his successors, Samuel Parrott (1788-1830) and Joseph Wilson (1787-1861) did not have a long history. In 1810, the congregation moved from Minster Street to take over a former Unitarian Chapel in London Street. Notwithstanding the Baptist element among its founder-members, new articles of belief, formulated in 1816, took a virulently paedo-Baptist stance. In spite of an interesting ministry among the Kennet bargees, numbers dwindled after Wilson's departure in 1827 and the remaining twelve members were received into the Broad Street fold. Neither of the two buildings occupied by the 'Salemites' remain today; their original home in Minster Street stood where now Heelas' pagoda-like premises imperiously dominate the skyline.

The Castle Street Chapel found difficulty in securing the services of a permanent Minister and had to rely on the ministrations of visiting preachers, who would usually come for a month or so or, as the Chapel Accounts have it, for three, four or five sabbaths. None of these gentlemen are household names today, though doubtless they were godly men in their times. Among them were: Messrs Brown, Bull, Cook, Drew, Gore, Jones, Kent, Leach, Marshall, Platt, Scott and Townsend; all of them proclaimed the Gospel of Christ in this place.

A major problem resulted from this varied diet: whereas Anglicans such as Gauntlett and partial conformists like William Green could be relied on to use the Book of Common Prayer, this was not the case with those belonging to other schools of nonconfirmity. The Committee's solution was a somewhat novel one. After Gauntlett's departure, the Chapel Clerk, Mr Joseph Watkins, had come to reside in the Chapel House, where he would entertain the visiting preachers. At a meeting of the Committee on 9 November 1808, 'a Motion was made by Mr Ring, seconded by Mr Swallow, — That from the inconvenience which has frequently arisen at the time of celebrating the Lord's Supper, (through disinclination of Ministers to use the form of the Established Church), it would be desirable for Mr Watkins to be ordained for that purpose'. This process took about six months, for it was recorded on 26 April 1809 that, 'Mr Watkins having according to the wish of the Committee been ordained', it was 'resolved that his expenses be paid to him with the best thanks and wishes of the Committee'. For many years he read the services in the Chapel, though he does not appear ever to have preached from its pulpit.

Watkins received what was termed an annuity, rather than a salary, of £65 per annum for his labours, which continued throughout James Sherman's ministry until his death in 1837. The Chapel Accounts for 1813 record the presentation to him of a silver teapot costing the princely sum of £13 16s. At his death he left £100 to be distributed among twenty poor communicants.

The Commitee was also concerned to prevent any recurrence of the misunderstanding of the Chapel's position that led to the schism of 1808. In 1810, therefore, they drew up a Trust Deed, designed to make clear their allegiance to the doctrine and orders of the Church of England. This document was to play an important part in the dispute over the transfer of the Chapel to Episcopal jurisdiction in 1836/7. The italicised portions are as highlighted in extracts quoted in a letter to the *Reading Mercury* in 1837 by Dr Ring and others:

'Whereas, a large body of people residing in the borough of Reading and its vicinity, who constantly attended the ministry of that zealous, learned, and indefatigable servant of God, the Honourable and Reverend William Bromley Cadogan, late Vicar of the parish of St Giles, in Reading aforesaid, well-known and approved in the sight of God and man, for his inflexible adherence to the pure doctrines of the Gospel as restored to our country by the Reformers, and contained in the Articles and Homilies of the Church of England, taken as they ever ought, and are commanded to be taken in their strict and literal meaning and acceptation *and being themselves also firmly and sincerely attached to the important doctrines and institutions of the Church, in which they were brought up,* and so fully instructed, finding also all hopes of profiting under the ministry of his successor disappointed, their endeavours to obtain a minister like-minded as their former pastor defeated, and yet *being as unwilling to depart from the government and discipline of the Church,* as they were determined by the grace of God, never to renounce its doctrines, or to listen to any other, they applied to each of the three Vicars of the parishes of Reading for permission to erect an Episcopal Chapel, vesting the appointment of the minister thereof in trustees, chosen by its founders, and being refused their reasonable request, they found themselves under the necessity of entering into a subscription among themselves, and erecting a chapel or building in Castle Street, in the parish of Saint Mary, in the town of Reading aforesaid, under the protection of the Toleration Act, *where they and their families might worship God according to the form prescribed in the Book of Common Prayer, and be instructed in the doctrines of the Church of England to which they had ever been accustomed, and thereby to prevent so large a body of people from dividing or incorporating themselves with such Dissenters or others, who, though they may hold the same evangelical doctrines as those contained in the Articles and Homilies of the Church of England, are unfriendly to the Ecclesiastical Establishment thereof, and inimical to the use and adoption of its form of prayer'.*

The Trustees, as we must now call them, were also anxious to protect the building from the secularisation that too often befell Nonconformist chapels, such as those in the Butts and Minster Street, when they fell into disuse. The deed, therefore, provided that if for seven years the building should have ceased to be used as a place of worship, it should be sold and, if all efforts to use the building or the proceeds of its sale for the activities of worship failed, the money obtained should be handed over to the London Missionary Society (LMS).

It may seem strange that such devoted Anglicans should have chosen the LMS as the beneificiary of last resort rather than the Church Missionary Society (CMS), of which

Reading-born Charles Simeon had been a founder. The reasons were possibly three-fold. Firstly, LMS began as a non-denominational body; its original Committee was composed of Anglicans, Church of Scotland, Methodists, Congregationalists and Presbyterians; as late as the 1830s this was part of its attraction to the young David Livingstone. Secondly, the Society had strong local connections, with both John Eyre and Archibald Douglas among its founding fathers. Finally, though CMS had come into being only four years after LMS, in 1799, it had been much slower in getting its missionary activities under way and was thus relatively little-known. In its first ten years, it had sent out only five missionaries, of whom one died and one was sacked whereas, by 1810 LMS was already active in the South Seas, China and the Indian sub-continent.

It was also in 1810 that an organist was added to the Chapel's payroll, a Mr Packer receiving £10 per annum for his musical efforts. Darter provides some interesting details of the Packer family:

'At the earliest period of my memory Mr Packer established a business in Minster Street as a watch-maker and jeweller . . .' He 'had a son who was educated as a musician and eventually became an organist at St Mary's Church. About the year 1815 he had a music shop in Minster Street, the front pilasters of which were adorned with gilt organ pipes. Mr Packer subsequently removed to a house in Castle Street and had a considerable amount of patronage as a teacher.'

If Packer junior was organist at the Butts church, was it his father, the jeweller, who played at Castle Street? Certainly, it was from him that the Chapel acquired the grand silver teapot presented to Joseph Watkins. He also made a modest contribution to the 1798 subscription for the building.

The decade from 1810 to 1820 was comparatively uneventful. Major repairs to the original building cost about £200 in 1816, but otherwise the preaching of the Gospel continued steadily sabbath by sabbath. The advent of the man who is arguably Castle Street's most celebrated Minister in 1820 heralds a new chapter.

Caversham Hll Chapel, founded by James Sherman. (ES)

JAMES SHERMAN — EARLY YEARS 1796-1830

James Sherman was only twenty-five years old when he accepted the call to minister at Castle Street. He was already becoming known as a preacher but, unlike his near contemporary, Henry Hart Milman, Vicar of St Mary's, he had no learned writings to his name, and indeed would not have claimed to be a man of great intellect or even natural gifts. His first attempt at extempore prayer had been a near-disaster and he suffered from recurrent throat problems that hindered his preaching ministry. Yet, as his biographer, Henry Allon, remarks, 'every gift becomes great when greatly consecrated', and this was surely true of James Sherman, of whom it was also said that the power of persuasion in his preaching was second only to that of George Whitefield himself, and that he scarcely ever proclaimed God's word without souls coming to faith in Christ.

He was born in 1796, at No 1, North Place, Banner Street, Finsbury, the son of a minor official in the East India Company. His parents were godly people; the mother had been converted while attending York Minster and the father under the ministry of John Newton at St Mary Woolnoth in the City of London. After receiving elementary education from Baptist and Anglican ministers, young James was apprenticed to an ivory-turner, making chess-pieces and billiard balls. Though a diligent lad, his heart was not in the work and his master was of the type whose interest in their employees was largely limited to the profits accruing from their labours.

James Sherman and his fellow-apprentices were worked from 6 am until 8 pm at the earliest and fed on a meagre diet, with meat only three times per week. James looked forward to the Lord's Day, which he would spend with his parents.

During this period, he was much affected by the preaching of a Mr King of Doncaster at Whitefield's Tabernacle in Tottenham Court Road. On one occasion, he heard him expound a text from Paul's sermon at Antioch in Pisidia, 'Be it known unto you men and brethren, that through this man is preached to you the forgiveness of sins'. (Acts 13.38) On his way thence, he seemed to hear a voice, saying, 'I am thy surety'. He 'felt that then and there God did literally "blot out my sins and doubt",' and 'went home rejoicing in His love'.

At the age of 16, he felt called to the ministry and sought his father's help in releasing him from his miserable bondage to the ivory-turner. At first, Mr Sherman was inclined to question his son's vocation but when a serious illness struck the lad down he was able to obtain the master's agreement to release him. Sherman received encouragement from Rev Robert Stodhart, Minister of Pell Street Chapel and, in spite of the setbacks which marked his first efforts, persistence won through. Lady Huntingdon's college had removed from Trevecca to Cheshunt in 1792 and it was here on 2 November 1815 that the nineteen-year old was enrolled as a probationary student.

Here the call to the ministry was confirmed; after three months, Sherman was commended for 'full admission, as a young man of fervent piety and possessing talents both for learning and preaching'. During his three years at Cheshunt College, he acquired preaching experience in the villages around London and further afield in Yarmouth and Norwich. Finally, on 26 November 1818 he was ordained at the Sion Chapel, Whitechapel, through the laying-on of hands by fellow-ministers which took the place of episcopal ordination in the Countess of Huntgindon's Connexion. His old pastor, Mr Stodhart, was one of those who took part.

The kind of supply-ministry on which Castle Street had relied was common among dissenting congregations then and thus it was that Sherman carried out a six-week stint in Devonport, before being attached on a more permanent basis to two of the Countess's chapels: first at Bath, then in Bristol where the effectiveness of his preaching was first observed. Within a short time the dwindling numbers attending began to revive. In Bristol, too, Sherman made the acquaintance of the now veteran Hannah More, and the wealthy and eccentric heiress, Mrs Schimmelpenninck, both of whom invited him to preach in their drawing rooms. Of this experience, he wrote, 'They introduced me to a class of society from which I derived much information and confidence'. It was also here that Sherman met his future wife, Miss Grant, whose 'piety and beauty soon won my heart'. At first, however, her father, Dr Grant, perhaps mindful of her tender age — she was six years younger than her suitor — was not at all predisposed to his prospective son-in-law!

It was during this period of courtship that the invitation reached James Sherman 'to become the pastor of a large and influential congregation in Reading'. A Mr Stoddart is recorded as having preached in Castle Street about this time and, if he is to be identified with Robert Stodhart, it is possible that he recommended his young friend to the Trustees. After consulting such friends as Rowland Hill and the Independent minister from Bath, William Jay, Sherman decided to come, as suggested, for a six-week probationary period. Although the exact date is not recorded, this probably commenced in September 1820.

Sherman's record of his first interview with the Trustees is worth recording in full — how well he observed them.

'My first interview with the elders of the church at Reading was at a dinner given for the purpose by Mr French. I think that I had never in one company seen so many fine heads:- Mr Tanner, a brewer, with his carefully-powdered hair and his queue, — Dr Ring, a physician, who had the leading practice in the town, remarkably handsome in countenance and elegant in manners, a most animated speaker and controversialist — Mr Stratton, who had been a bookseller in London, with a complexion as fair as a lily although he was seventy, powdered and trim, with a head that would have made a fine subject for the crayons of Russell [vi], — Mr French, a refined and well-informed man, with a singularly benevolent countenance, and one of the most heavenly-minded men with whom I ever came in contact, — Mr Compeigne, an attorney, precise and elegant in all his belongings, with sharp features and a well-shaped head, — Mr Baylis, the clerk of St Giles' Church for the last thirty years, gentlemanly in his manners, and a superior man in intelligence and piety, Mr Billing, a younger man, a builder, and some others".

'With one or two exceptions', adds Sherman, 'these were all the fruits of Mr Cadogan's ministry, and were men of peculiar godliness'. He also remarks on their longevity: 'it became a proverb that if you wanted a good lease of your life, you must become a member of the Committee of Castle Street Chapel'.

On this first occasion, Sherman also made a good impression on the Committee, especially on Dr Ring who, observing his abstemiousness at dinner, remarked: 'My young friend, I was very glad to see you could let the bottle pass after two glasses'.

The probationary period seems to have been largely a matter of form; but if there were any who doubted that Sherman's appointment was according to the will of God, these must have been dispelled by the record of those six weeks. 'Testimonials of acceptance came in the form of crowded congregations and some hopeful proofs of conversion to God'.

Above all it was his sermon during the great Reading Cheese Fair that firmly established the young preacher's reputation. This event was held in the Forbury every Michaelmas and was the largest market of its kind in the country; the quantity of cheese on sale usually ranged from 500 to 800 tons, with a record of 1200 set in 1795.

'Long before the doors [of the chapel] were opened', we read, 'the crowd stretched across the road, and as soon as an entrance could be obtained, a general rush took place.' Used as we are to congregations dawdling into church at the last moment, it is scarcely possible to imagine such a scene!

Sherman had chosen the text from Romans, 6.21: 'The end of these things is death'. After showing how fairs had changed from their original worthy purpose to becoming vehicles for sinful and degrading activities, he powerfully brought the theme home to the individual and his sinful state, preaching for one and a half hours till at last exhaustion forced him to desist. The congregation was, of course, made up of folk from many different parts of the land, and Sherman remarks that he 'seldom took a journey from home without meeting someone' whose religious awakening had dated from that service.

Sherman began his official pastorate on 15 April 1821, choosing as his text some of Moses' parting words of blessing to the Twelve Tribes of Israel: 'As thy days, so shall thy strength be'. (Deut. 33.25) Dr Ring recalled these words when saying farewell to Sherman fifteen years later, when perhaps they seemed more appropriate to the occasion: 'If you preach as you have done amongst us, you need not tell the people where your strength came from. I am an old man, you in the vigour of manhood; but you can do no more than I, except Christ strengthen you'.

Sherman's fame spread fast so that every sitting in the Chapel was soon let and the aisles filled to overflowing at almost every service. Not all, however, were willing hearers. We are told of one gentleman from London, a senior Government official, who was visiting Reading with his wife to arrange the education of their children. He at first declined to accompany her to the service, but later out of curiosity followed her steps to the Chapel. Intrigued by the absence of empty seats he stayed to hear Sherman preach on the text, 'A little that a righteous man hath is better than the riches of the wicked' (Ps. 37.16), and went away, a disciple of Christ.

In 1823, the Chapel celebrated its 25th anniversary. On this occasion, Sherman confined his preaching to the afternoon service, while Castle Street's good old friend, Rowland Hill, now advanced in years, preached morning and evening. Once again people were found queuing up 'long before the hours of service'. The Jubilee was marked by a further harvest of souls and at the same time was celebrated in practical terms by the installation of gas lighting, then rather a novelty in Reading.

At first Sherman used to write out his sermons, commit them to memory and then deliver them without reference to notes. However, this practice caused him considerable mental strain and contributed to the severe breakdown which he suffered in 1826. He was obliged to retire to Clifton for a few months and, after his return, adopted the more usual practice of writing and preaching from notes.

Although most of Sherman's publications date from the period after he left Reading, a series of sermons preached to the Castle Street congregation was published in 1826 as *A Guide to Acquaintance with God*. An extract from this may serve as a sample of Sherman's style; we can see here how firmly the Cross was at the centre of his preaching:
'The cross is the centre of all God's purposes of mercy to fallen man, around which they shine with so resplendent a lustre that they eclipse all other systems intended to lighten

man into the secret places of the Almighty. If you therefore sincerely desire to be a friend to God, and to live habitually in his favour, Christ's atonement must be the basis on which your hopes are raised. He causes all his love to settle on his Son, and you must fix on him also. He is well pleased with the work of his Son, and you must be satisfied in it too . . . He has set him forth as the brazen serpent was exhibited by Moses, that you might behold his virtues, and, looking on him, live'.

Apart from the steady work in Reading Town Centre, the extension of Christ's Kingdom to the surrounding villages was also an important feature of Sherman's ministry. We have already seen how this motivated Peter French to found the chapel at Peppard. Daughter chapels to Castle Street had been founded at Sonning in 1805/7 and at Pound Green (near Grazeley), the latter of uncertain date. After returning from the enforced rest at Clifton, 'I now,' wrote Sherman, 'turned my special attention to a more ample provision for preaching the gospel in the villages around Reading'.

This work often began with meetings 'held in the kitchens of farmers, and other friends willing to bear the odium of such services', but wherever possible a chapel was built as a focal point for the Gospel work. The first was at Woodley, a generous gift of £50 leading to other donations which enabled 'a very pretty little church, holding about two hundred persons, built of Bath stone, with small tower and steeple' to be 'erected for little more than £300'. Up to this date, it seems, the village of Woodley was noted for the part that poaching played in its black economy; so effective was the preaching in curbing this activity that the Squire was accustomed to present the local evangelist with an annual gift of game as a thanks-offering!

Caversham Hill followed in 1827. Services were held at a farmhouse until an elderly friend of Rowland Hill, Mrs Burchett, made available some land near Emmer Green, saying to Sherman that she 'would like to build a house of God if you will undertake it'. She later provided the Chapel with an endowment of £1,500. During its early years, Caversham Hill Chapel was nicknamed Black Horse Chapel after an inn that stood next to it.

Theale at the time had an unenviable reputation. It was known proverbially as 'Little Sodom' and one minister who had attempted to preach in this village of the plain was hooted at and pelted, till he had no choice but to turn tail. Sherman's determination to succeed where others had failed was for a while thwarted; even the few converted folk, like Lot of old, were too frightened of their lawless neighbours to allow the use of their homes and spare land proved impossible to find, as the local landowners were much opposed to anything that smacked of dissent. Eventually, a brave butcher, who had been converted at Castle Street, provided his kitchen for services; the land problem was finally solved by erecting a chapel in his garden.

The last two chapels were those built at Binfield Heath and Wargrave, both opened in 1835. Of the former, seating 250, Sherman wrote: 'Beautiful is the landscape, but far more beautiful as a place where men were transformed into living temples for the living God'. At its opening service, Rev George Clayton of Walworth harangued the villagers in these terms:
'O ye who are thoughtless and careless for your souls' eternal good, give a moment, at least, to reflection, and ask how it is that others should . . . expend thought, and time, and property, and prayer — on building for you a house of worship, and others coming sabbath after sabbath, through the winter's storms and the summer's heat, to teach you the good way of the Lord; and you all stupour and indifference, making no movement towards heaven, nor ever urging the question, "What must I do to be saved?"'.

Wargrave was another village noted for its opposition to the Gospel. One preacher, sent from Henley, had had to face 'drowning his voice by noises and endangering his life by missiles of every description'. The money to provide for the chapel building was raised through a rather unlikely means for an Evangelical church, certainly of those days — by a village bazaar! Sherman was clearly uneasy, but when the word went out from the ungodly to boycott this fund-raising event he took the view that if in this instance such opposition could be overcome by prayer and determination it would be a witness to the Gospel. It seems that everyone of his flock was under a three-line whip to attend and the £300 needed to build the Chapel was duly raised.

Some of these village tabernacles have disappeared and that at Wargrave closed for worship as recently as 1981. That at Woodley has recently been converted into an estate agents' office. Binfield Heath and Caversham Hill, however, are still flourishing as independent evangelical churches. One remarkable feature of them is the use of a simplified Gothic architectural style, something, as Pevsner has noted, almost unheard of in dissenting chapels of the period and perhaps an indication of their 'partial conformist' connections. After the disruption of 1836, they all remained under nonconformist control and for the time being church-planning from Castle Street ceased, to be revived in the 1960s.

Forbury, where Reading Cheese Fair was held — the occasion when
James Sherman made his mark. (CB)

41

James Sherman, Minister 1821-36.

JAMES SHERMAN — LATER YEARS 1830-1862

Sherman had finally succeeded in overcoming Dr Grant's opposition to his marriage. Moved more by the distress of his daughter than the entreaties of his prospective son-in-law, the Doctor had given consent to their wedding, which took place at St Nicholas, Bristol in January 1822. Dr Grant learnt at last to respect his daughter's spouse and in their later years he and his wife moved to Reading.

Thus it came about that the early 1830s were marked by great personal sorrow for James Sherman through the deaths of those dear to him. In rapid succession he lost first his own beloved parents, then his father-in-law and on New Year's Day, 1834, his wife, whose health had been much weakened by the birth of their third child. She was much loved by the congregation and had played her own part in the ministry, particularly as Secretary of the Infants Friend Society, an organisation which, in Consterdine's words, conferred 'invaluable benefit on the mothers of the poorer class'. Finally, her brother, Edwin, a young man of delicate health, of whom Sherman had become fond, was also called home.

Mrs Sherman and Dr Grant were buried in the ground outside the Chapel in an area later enclosed by the extensions of 1840. The Trustees consulted Sherman, whether the bodies should be reinterred elsewhere. He was content for them to remain where they were, provided they were not disturbed by the building works; even so a cupboard under the staircase leading up to the Gallery is hardly a dignified place of rest.

The Trustees had retained their loyalty to the Church of England during the twenty years since the compilation of the Trust Deed and in 1831 a fresh attempt was made to regularise the situation. Such a move may have been facilitated by the appointment in 1825 of a Bishop of Salisbury who was sympathetic to the Evangelical cause. Thomas Burgess (1756-1837) had previously been Bishop of St Davids where he had worked hard at reforming the diocese and improving the quality of his clergy; to the latter end he had established Lampeter College. He was also a founder of the Bible Society, a promoter of Sunday schools, a campaigner against Unitarianism and associate of Hannah More. An interesting quirk of Bishop Burgess — arising from his Celtic exile — was an obsession with the alleged origin of the British Church in a missionary journey of St Paul unrecorded in Scripture.

Sherman was content that an approach should be made to the Bishop and was indeed prepared to consider entering Anglican orders himself. His own parents had been converted under the ministry of the Established Church and like others of the Countess of Huntingdon's Connexion he had no quarrels with Anglican doctrine or liturgy. He modified this position later in life, contending that the independence of the local congregation was preferable to dependence on church endowments: (writing in the 1840s) 'I believe that no congregation prospers like that which supports its own minister, and cheerfully aids the cause of God to the utmost of its ability'.

The first attempt to bring the period of partial conformity to a close was thwarted as a result of the line taken by the vicar of St Mary's. Henry Hart Milman (1791-1868) is best-known today as the author of that thrilling Palm Sunday hymn, *Ride on, Ride on in Majesty,* composed like most of his hymnody, during his eighteen years in Reading. In his own day, he was better known for his historical writings, such as the *History of the Jews,* published in 1829, and his later *History of Latin Christianity.* Milman went on to become, in 1835, Vicar of St Margaret's, Westminster, and later Dean of St Paul's.

Milman's terms were unacceptable to the Trustees. He wanted the Chapel to be fully consecrated rather than merely licensed as a place of worship; he demanded that he and his successors should have right of veto on the presentation to the incumbency; and (perhaps the major sticking-point) he required a change in the composition of the Trustees, with the overall number reduced and with the ex-officio inclusion of various members of the hierarchy, including the Bishop of the Diocese, the Archdeacon and the Vicar of St Mary's. Such an arrangement would surely have threatened the continuity of the Evangelical ministry which the Trust Deed was designed to guarantee.

Following the breakdown of negotiations, Sherman appears to have discarded for all time the possibility of episcopal ordination. Not long after the death of his first wife, another door began to open for him. The occasion of this was another death, that of Rowland Hill in 1833, and the consequent vacancy in the pastorate of the Surrey Chapel. Sherman had occasionally preached there during Hill's lifetime and the late minister had expressed the wish that his young friend might succeed him. In October 1834, Sherman accepted an invitation to supply the pulpit for six weeks during his annual vacation.

Rowland Hill had been admitted to deacon's orders but refused ordination to the priesthood by the Archbishop of York on account of his itinerating tendency. Some of his most powerful preaching had been in St George's Fields, Southwark, at the time of the Gordon Riots of 1780; two years later the Surrey Chapel was erected for him there. Though built for a stranded minister rather than a stray congregation and octagonal in design, it resembled the Castle Street Chapel in its form of government, in that its ownership 'was vested in the hands of fifteen trustees, its doctrinal basis the articles of the Church of England, and its pulpit free to pious ministers of all denominations'. Lady Huntingdon's biographer quotes an American traveller as stating the probability that 'no place of worship has been the source of more institutions for promoting the glory of God'. Alas, Surrey Chapel is no longer to be seen; after suffering the kind of ignominy the Trustees of Castle Street sought to avoid — alternative use as boxing ring — it finally succumbed to one of Hitler's bombs in the raids of 1940.

Sherman's ministry at the Chapel in 1834 had two important results. The first was an invitation — hardly unexpected in view of Hill's recorded wishes — to the permanent ministry. Though clearly attracted by the offer, Sherman was moved by concern for the effect his moving might have on his present flock: 'the prosperous state of the church and congregation at Reading, and its liability to be scattered upon my leaving' influenced his initial decision to decline the invitation from the Surrey Trustees.

The second, less predictable, outcome was the advent of the second Mrs Sherman. It was while supplying the Surrey pulpit during those six weeks that James Sherman met Martha, daughter of Mr Benjamin Tucker of Enfield, whom he married in March 1835.

Although Martha Sherman spent only eighteen months in Reading, she made a notable impact on the life of the community, particularly through visiting the poor in Coley, where 'children would greet her and people threw open their doors to receive their "friend", as they delighted to call her'. In the *Memoir* Sherman wrote after her death in 1848, he says that 'in twelve months' labour, the locality assumed an air of greater cleanliness and comfort, many of its inhabitants attended the preaching of the gospel — every child capable of leaving home was sent to a Sunday School, and some few instances of hopeful conversion, were the high reward of this disinterested labour of love'.

The Shermans lived in the Chapel House, the last ministerial family to do so until the Burnetts in the 1920s; Mrs Sherman was much taken with its qualities as a desirable residence, describing it in a letter to a friend as 'very dry and healthy and, as you would expect, very nicely furnished'.

When a second call from the Surrey Chapel came to Sherman eighteen months after the first, the situation in Reading had altered considerably. The state of the Anglican church was at last showing signs of a change for the better. This process had begun in 1827 with the founding of Holy Trinity as an episcopal proprietary chapel with George Hulme as its first incumbent; its Evangelical origins would scarcely be imagined by a 'Stranger in Reading' today!

1834 saw the arrival at St Giles of John Cecil Grainger, a man of moderately Evangelical views. He appointed as his Curate a staunch Evangelical named Francis Trench who married a daughter of William Marsh and built the daughter church of St John's, Watlington Street, at his own expense in 1837. At St Laurence's, the work laid down by William Marsh in 1811 was taken up in 1835 by Rev John Ball (1799-1865). Finally when, in the same year, Henry Hart Milman took his leave of Reading to minister to the spiritual needs of the Lords and Commons, his successor, Samuel Wildman Yates, thought not himself an Evangelical, proved to be a much more cooperative character.

As a result of all these changes, the dispersal of the Castle Street congregation feared by Sherman began to happen; some of those whose loyalty to the Establishment exceeded their affection for the Castle Street Chapel began to frequent those older churches where a Biblical ministry was once more available. The ageing Trustees were, therefore, determined to stem the tide by a fresh effort to secure episcopal recognition.

Sherman after much prayer came to the conviction that the Lord was indeed leading him to the ministry of Surrey Chapel. Not everyone, however, was prepared to accept his decision. A rather cantankerous wealthy old lady, named Mrs Adams, who lived next to the Chapel House, 'had taken it into her head that he had made a promise binding himself never to leave Reading as long as she lived'.

Not only had she augmented Sherman's income by £100 a year and contributed substantially to the building costs of the Binfield Heath Chapel, but under her will she had also bequeathed him a sum in excess of £2,000, together with £1,500 for each of the three Sherman children. When finally all pleas to the Minister to remain proved of no avail, she cast the will into the fire and told him that she did not wish to see him again until the day of judgement! Sherman commented on this episode as follows: 'I confess that for a short time the struggle was great; but when I considered that the inducement was merely an increase of wealth, and that, so far as I could judge, the voice of God called me to Surrey, I dared not hesitate'.

After visiting all the village outstations to encourage the faithful, Sherman took his leave of Castle Street on 28 August 1836. His valedictory sermon was on the text from the second Epistle of St John: 'Look to yourselves, that we lose not those things which we have wrought, but that we receive a full reward'.

His ministry at the Surrey Chapel was equally blessed with a great harvest of souls. Attendances increased from 550 to over 1,400 in the first ten years; 257 of these, many of them new converts, were added during 1837. At one service during that year, there were 84 professions of new-found faith. Failing health led him to resign in 1854, but even then we find him taking on the challenge of a new Congregational Chapel at Blackheath, and soon attracting around 1,000 hearers. Towards the end of his life, he travelled abroad to Egypt and Malta and even made the acquaintance of the King of Prussia to whom the fame of his preaching had spread. The final home-call came, after a long period of physical decline, on 15 February 1862.

At the time of his death, one long-standing member of the Castle Street congregation wrote of James Sherman: 'Nearly thirty years have passed since he left us and few are remaining of his people. This I can testify, never did any minister more gain the hearts of his people than he. His sermons sent us home to our closets, and made us careful to harrow in the good seed of the word before the birds of the air had time to rob us of it.'

Neither did Reading forget the preacher who had stirred the hearts of so many of its residents and visitors. In the mid-'70s, one of the new roads in Katesgrove was named Sherman Road. The author of this book is proud to live there.

Sherman was a prolific writer, especially after leaving Reading. Apart from his unfinished *Memoirs*, edited by his friend, Henry Allon, and his tribute to Martha Sherman, *The Pastor's Wife*, they included numerous sermons and memorial addresses, commentaries on Ezekiel and Philippians, temperance tracts and a preface to the first British edition of *Uncle Tom's Cabin*.

In spite of his clearly stated preference for congregational independence Sherman remained friendly to the Anglican church, and to any in which the Word of God was preached; to one young man with Anglican sympathies who had enquired whether he would be welcome at the Lord's Table, he wrote: 'My chief desire is not to impoverish other churches of their members, but to gain the World to Christ, and make saints of sinners' — a cardinal rule, surely, for all who would preach the Gospel.

*Acquaint and be
now thyself at peace
with God.* Job xii, 21.

ERECTED BY THE CONGREGATION
IN MEMORY OF THEIR FORMER PASTOR

THE REV. JAMES SHERMAN
WITH PERSUASIVE EARNESTNESS
AND HONOURED BY HIS DIVINE MASTER WITH GREAT USEFULNESS
HE MINISTERED IN THE SURREY CHAPEL
AS THE SUCCESSOR TO THE REV. ROWLAND HILL
FROM 1836 TO 1854
AND ENTERED INTO THE JOY OF HIS LORD, 15TH FEBRUARY, 1862
AGED 66 YEARS

*'THEY THAT TURN MANY TO RIGHTEOUSNESS SHALL SHINE AS THE
STARS FOR EVER AND EVER'* — DAN. xii.3.

Memorial erected to James Sherman at Surrey Chapel

PALTRY PROCEEDINGS 1836

Plans to transfer the Chapel to the Church of England had been laid some time before Sherman's departure but could not be fulfilled while the dissenting Minister remained in office.

At a meeting of the Trustees on 19 July, at which Sherman's resignation was accepted, Dr Ring reported on the encouragement he had received from an informal conversation with Mr Yates; eight days later, the Trustees agreed by six votes to five to commence discussions with the authorities. George Hulme of Trinity Chapel played his part by acting as an envoy from the Trustees to the Bishop.

Events moved quickly after Sherman's removal. Four days after his valedictory Sunday, on Thursday 1 September, Thomas Ring was able to show his fellow Trustees the licence from the Bishop of Salisbury authorizing the use of the Chapel for Church of England services. Old Mr Tanner, now resident in Bath, was among those present and expressed his 'full concurrence' with the turn of events. The Trustees then joined with the congregation — and some 14 or 15 sympathetic clergymen — in a special service of Evening Prayer, 'the first held under the new condition of things', as James Consterdine puts it.

Dr Ring had invited Charles Simeon to make the journey from Cambridge to preach on the occasion, but he did not feel equal to the task; the end of his earthly labours was indeed only a few months away. His gracious letter of regret can be found appended to his *Memoirs*. 'I happen to know the differences between 37 and 77; and I am content to discharge, as God shall enable me, the offices pertaining to the latter age . . . It is a real joy to me also to see that Church, to which I am very deeply attached, prospering by the return of some of *her best-loved friends* to her Communion'.

William Marsh, now Rector of St Thomas, Birmingham, proved to be an excellent second choice and in the view of one of the Trustees, quoted in the *Mercury,* preached 'a most impressive sermon'. The prayers were read by Rev Peter French, Vicar of Holy Trinity, Burton-on-Trent. At the first Sunday service, the preacher was Professor James Scholefield (1789-1853), Regius Professor of Greek at Cambridge and a noted polemicist against the Tractarians, who had served a curacy under Simeon.

Charles Simeon's favourable sentiments were by no means shared by all the congregation. An apparently innocuous notice that appeared in the *Mercury* on 6 August, to the effect that Sherman would preach for a further three Sundays and then the Church would be '*consecrated* for the services of the Church of England', evoked a number of strongly-worded letters from those who opposed the action of the Trustees. In spite of the efforts of the Committee which drew up the Trust Deed in 1810, ignorance of the Anglican origins of the congregation was still widespread, nor was it readily appreciated that the agreement with the Diocese and the Vicar of St Mary's granted the appointment of the Minister to the Trustees *perpetually.* Thus, 'A Cadoganite' writing on 20 August:

'No circumstance has of late years excited deeper regret than the resolution of the majority of the Trustees to assign this chapel to the exclusive service of the Church of England. The *certainty* of the Gospel being preached is now to pass out of their hands . . . Allowing that, according to their novel plan of selection, one of the many candidates for the pulpit may appear eligible at present, where is the security that the Gospel is to be preached, that the whole counsel of God is always to be brought forth? Because the Trustees having once nominated a Minister and the Bishop having inducted him, he is quite out of the control of the Trustees, and whatever doctrine he may preach, they have no power of saying aye or no.'

Other letters refer to a memorial drawn up by 250 members opposed to the planned change, with accusations that the Trustees (rather in the manner of the young Cadogan) had treated this with 'silent contempt' and had alleged that its signatories were 'only a pack of mere boys and old women'. The Trustees seem to have largely held their peace at this stage, perhaps in the vain hope that silence would defuse the situation. Eventually the controversy did blow over to be replaced in the public eye by arguments over the merits of abolishing church rates, but not before the dissidents had taken irrevocable steps to go their own way.

On 6 September, a meeting attended by 200 took place at Broad Street Chapel under the chairmanship of the Baptist leader, John Howard Hinton (1791-1873), then Minister of the new Kings Road Baptist Church built for the former Hosier Lane assembly and later Secretary of the Baptist Union. It was resolved to form 'a new Congregation in Reading on Dissenting principles', the pretext being as follows:
'The Church party having now effected their principles by a practical measure of so decided a character (ie the intended consecration of the Chapel for Anglican worship), consistency requires that those who are not Churchmen should assert theirs.'

The new Congregation commenced its worship in temporary premises in Bridge Street hired from Messrs Musgrove and Quelch, at the end of the month, with Rev Jesse Hopwood of Chelsea supplying the first two Sabbaths. A permanent site was soon acquired, almost opposite the new congregation's former Chapel, on the south side of Castle Street. The new building, erected at a cost of £3,500 and capable of seating 900 to 1,000, was opened in October 1837; that animosity towards their former friends remained can be seen from the following Notice that appeared in the *Mercury* on 21 October:
'The Congregational Chapel of Castle Street is now completed, and will be opened for Divine Service on Wednesday next. It is a very elegant building, and reflects great credit upon the taste and abilities of Mr Cooper, the architect. The opening sermon will be delivered by the Rev J. Sherman, [vii] the late beloved and excellent Minister of the Place of Worship, now yclept St Mary's Chapel, of which this numerous and highly respectable portion of our Dissenting brethren, for upwards of 30 years, held possesion, but of which by means of the most paltry proceedings, they have recently been deprived.'

Though the Trustees of that other place of worship had hitherto shown restraint, they now felt compelled to defend their honour. In a letter to the *Mercury*, dated 1 November and signed by Thomas Ring, Joseph Young and Robert Lawrance, they detailed at length the reasons why those who wished to dissent from the Established Church had no legal right to possession of the Castle Street Chapel, with liberal quotations from the Trust Deed. Perhaps the most telling argument was that of the £2,000 required to pay for the Chapel only three guineas had been contributed by dissenters! This letter seems to have been effective in scotching any further criticism of the Trustees' conduct, though there were three notable defections from their ranks during 1838. Thomas Willats and Peter French resigned of their own accord (though there is no evidence of their joining the new

Congregation), but a Mr Bourne had to be voted off, 'he having joined a new society' and 'acted contrary to the tenour and effects of' the Trust Deed. It is assumed that he is the same Mr Bourne appointed a Trustee of the new Chapel in March 1837.

Castle Street Congregational Chapel flourished under its first pastor, Mr Spedding Curwen (1790-1856) and remained in use as a church until 1956 when failing attendances, town centre depopulation and the forbidding cost of major repairs brought about its closure, with many of the members transferring their energies to a new church on the Southcote estate. The building was until recently in use as a furniture shop but has now been transformed into an entertainment complex, comprising a gymnasium, restaurant and night club — thus catering for some of the prevailing objects of 'worship' in our secular society.

The split-up of his former congregation, of which he had been so fearful, seems to have wounded Sherman deeply. In his preface to a *Memoir of Rowland Hill,* published in 1837 when the Castle Street situation would have been very much on his mind, he wrote: 'For my own part, I should hail the day which would afford my beloved brethren in the Establishment, full liberty to preach the unsearchable riches of Christ at Surrey Chapel, without offending any ecclesiastical law, even although I might still be shut out of their pulpits . . . I add my earnest wishes . . . that our Saviour's prayer will ere long be accomplished. "That they all may be one . . ."' A letter written by Sherman on 17 September 1836 is further evidence of the regret he clearly felt:

'It would have afforded me more pleasure if the Congregation over whom it was my privilege to labour for nearly sixteen years had continued united but knowing that the transfer of the Chapel to the Establishment by the Trustees interferes with the conscientious views of a large number who have been accustomed to worship there, I beg to commend them to the notice of those of my esteemed Brethren whom they may invite to labour among them.'

It is possible to read a happy ending to this painful story of schism by referring to accounts of the funeral of Spedding Curwen. The pall-bearers included George Tubbs, incumbent of St Mary's, Castle Street, as well as Cecil Grainger of St Giles and Francis Trench of St John's, evidence that by the 1850s Evangelicals within and without the Establishment were able to unite in the cause of the Gospel.

Although it has been said — by Sherman's biographer — that the 'building went one way and the congregation went another', it is not possible to quantify the split exactly. Others have spoken of a substantial minority crossing the road to the new Chapel and this is corroborated by the numbers of admissions to membership recorded in its Minute Book which numbered about 130 before the arrival of Mr Curwen in 1838. In their letter of 1 November, the Trustees of the Episcopal Chapel referred to 'the steps lately taken with happy effect', a clause from which Consterdine has drawn the plausible conclusion that episcopal recognition had brought back into the fold some of those who had defected to other Anglican congregations.

The Trustees were also happy in their choice of the first incumbent under the new order. Charles James Goodhart was among a number of candidates already under consideration prior to Sherman's departure. At first he was a little hesitant about making the move: 'When I look at myself I feel I am really so incompetent that I only wonder the Lord has not got rid of me long ago'. Like Sherman, Goodhart at first came on a probationary basis. He is to be found in Reading as early as 17 September, when his presence was noted at a meeting of the Berkshire Association of the CMS, addressed by the apostle of South America, Captain Allen Gardner, though his invitation to preach for two Sabbaths dates from the end of that month. The *Mercury* on 5 November informed its readers 'that the Rev Mr Goodhart who preached at Castle Street Chapel a few weeks since with so much acceptance, is expected again on Sunday next to preach the morning and evening of that day.'

The following day, the Trustees resolved to invite him to take up the ministry and on the 9th Goodhart wrote accepting with his customary humility: 'knowing the grace, mercy and peace which the Lord has so abundantly in store and fully believing that I am coming among a praying people, I take courage and throw myself on Him who is able to do exceedingly abundantly above all that we can ask or think.'

Born in 1804, Charles James Goodhart had been a scholar at Trinity College, Cambridge, where in 1826, he came out as 22nd Wrangler and took 4th place in the 2nd Class of the Classical Tripos. It is likely that while at Trinity he would have come under the pervasive influence of Charles Simeon. Following ordination in 1827, he held curacies at Haselbury-Bryan, Dorset and (from 1831) at Broad Chalke, Wiltshire.

Towards the end of his long life, in September 1839, Dr Ring wrote of God's providential dealings with the congregation in relation to the appointment of the new Minister, recalling those words of scripture that had reassured them in 1797:

'The Revd James Sherman . . . gave up his charge over the flock of Castle Street Chapel after [blank] years of faithful . . . labours amongst them . . . The great Head of the Church mercifully sent us another most excellent in the Revd C. J. Goodhart . . . *Jesus Xt is the same, yesterday, today and for ever.* He has said, "Fear not I am with you always".'

William Marsh preached the first sermon in the Chapel after it was
joined to the Establishment.

Castle Street Congregational Church, founded in 1837. (BLAT)

Castle Street, showing the two chapels on either side. (BLAT)

FIRST YEARS OF EPISCOPACY 1836-1852

At first, it had been the intention of the Trustees that the church should be consecrated, but two attempts to proceed with this in 1840 and in 1846 were abandoned, chiefly as a result of the complications caused by the reversionary interest of the London Missionary Society.

In the second instance, the Bishop ruled that consecration could proceed if the Society was prepared to waive its rights. The Directors of LMS were sympathetic and clearly felt that the likelihood of any benefit to the Society was remote; however, as officers elected for one year only, they did not feel competent to bind their successors. Initial steps were taken to engineer the Act of Parliament needed to alter the Trust Deed but these were deferred because of an imminent General Election and eventually abandoned because of the expense.

Consecration, in the sense used here 'is a legal act conveying the property to the Church of England for all time'. The Trustees' failure to attain their object does not, therefore, affect the building's spiritual consecration as a place of worship; William Stubbs, church historian and Bishop of Oxford (1888-1901), is recorded as saying to Consterdine, 'The fact of your reading the service in it really consecrates it'.

It had been originally intended that the building should be designated Cadogan Chapel, and indeed the old minute-book of the Trustees, now lodged in Shire Hall, is entitled 'Minutes of Cadogan Chapel'. Though this name is found as late as 1852 in Goodhart's letter of resignation, the alternative, St Mary's Chapel, is in one of the 1836/7 letters to the *Mercury,* whereas in their letter of 1 November 1837, the Trustees refer to Castle Street (Episcopal) Chapel. The expression, St Mary's Episcopal Chapel, appears in a minute of 1840 and this became the generally accepted legal description, shortened in the revised Trust Deed of 1856 to St Mary's Chapel.

Consterdine tells of a simple lady who, on being twitted by her friends for going to chapel, responded vehemently, 'I'se neither Church nor Chapel, I'se 'Piscopy'! Possibly as a result of the confusion that arose with the Parish Church, the present usual description of St Mary's, Castle Street, eventually prevailed.

Folowing the departure of Mr and Mrs Sherman, the Chapel House was for a while occupied by their former housemaid, Hannah Hearn. This remarkable lady was still alive aged 93 years in 1898, when she took part in the opening service of a new chapel at Toker's Green, near Caversham, close to her birthplace. From 1842, it was occupied by a new Chapel Clerk, Stephen Brown, who was destined for service equally long and distinguished as that rendered by Joseph Watkins; his tenure of the premises was marked by the, no doubt welcome, installation of a water closet.

Abraham Armstrong held the office of Clerk after the death of Watkins and died aged 75 in September of 1842. Apart from his clerical activities he was Visitor to the 'Sick Man's Friend' for 40 years.

Goodhart, perhaps as befitted a Church of England clergyman, occupied a rather grander residence at Holy Brook House, further up Castle Street. Here he augmented his salary by taking in pupils, one of whom, Alfred Christopher, described the house as an 'especially fine mid-18th century mansion'.

Christopher (1820-1913) spent three months with Goodhart in 1839, before going up to Cambridge; listening to Goodhart's preaching, 'he often felt unhappy that he was not converted'. Happily for the Church of England, Goodhart's work was continued by Simeon's successor, William Carus, and Christopher went on to become a distinguished Rector of St Aldate's, Oxford, where he ministered for 46 years. He and Goodhart became life-long friends, with his old mentor a frequent visitor to Oxford in later years.

In December 1839, the decision was taken to give the Chapel a more dignified external appearance; whether this was in response to the possibly grander façade of the new chapel over the road we cannot tell. The architects chosen were the brothers, Henry and Nathaniel Briant, who had also designed the Royal Berkshire Hospital and were probably, therefore, well-known to those of the Trustees, such as Dr Ring, who had been involved with that project. Their plans were preferred to those of John (?) Billing and J. B. Clacy. The work was completed in 1840 for some £800 and the chancel added shortly after. H. Godwin Arnold has described the architectural features as follows:

'The Chapel was originally a simple Georgian style building, but in 1840 a hexastyle temple front in the Greek Corinthian style was added, crowned by a narrow turret using the order from the Tower of the Winds in Athens . . . The temple front, and the rather meagre 'pepper pot' — and one might add, the sober 'neat' interior — typify almost everything that Pugin most loathed in Church design. It none the less remains one of the best Church interiors in Reading and the portico is an ornament to what is left of the street.'

The 'pepper-pot' reference is to a less complimentary description of the new belfry penned by a local rhymer:-

> 'And then there's that good-hearted man,
> Who preaches to the people,
> Where Briant built a pepper box,
> And called it a steeple.'

He would doubtless have been pleased to learn that the loathsome pepper-box was removed in the 1950s for safety reasons, leaving the rather odd effect of its truncated base.

The choice of the Corinthian Order for the columns is an unusual feature. The Ionic order, with its scroll-like capitals, is far more common in the churches of the Greek Revival, had been used by the Briants at the Royal Berks and is indeed to be found in the interior of the chapel. The architects may have felt that the elaborate leafy capitals would provide a suitable contrast to the simple Doric Order of the new chapel opposite.

Henry Briant (1813-84) retired from architecture shortly after his work in Castle Street to study at Cambridge, following which he was ordained. He was for many years Vicar of Macclesfield, where he was assisted by one of Tubbs' former curates, Gordon Smyth. There is, however, some evidence, though not conclusive, that it was his brother, Nathaniel, who was largely responsible for the Castle Street façade; all the references in the Trustees' minutes are to Mr Briant.

Further additions to St Mary's Castle Street's 'plant' were made during the Goodhart era, with the addition of the two-storey School Room and the present vestry and organ-housing, flanking both sides of the chancel. At a lower level of activity, the Trustees resolved in 1841 that 'Mr Lodge be requested to fix proper scrapers at the chapel doors'.

The addition of the School Room facilitated the development of a flourishing Sunday School. A Minute-Book of Teachers' Meetings, dating from 1847-60, includes discussions on behavioural problems and illiteracy. The scholarly Goodhart took a keen interest in this work and sought to guide the teachers towards the most effective methods of presenting the Gospel.

The affable Mr Yates was accommodating to his 'chapels of ease' and both Charles Goodhart and William Phelps of Trinity were given permission to exercise a local ministry in parts of his parish. In Goodhart's case, the area of ministry was clearly Coley, where Mrs Sherman's endeavours were still remembered with affection.

The new Clerk and Scripture Reader, Stephen Brown, was largely identified with the work in Coley, to the extent that he was frequently known locally as 'Parson Brown' and even 'Bishop of Coley'. In April 1853, the Trustees resolved that his 'salary as Clerk and Collector of Pew Rents be increased to Twenty (£20) Pounds per annum'. After being given notice to quit the Chapel House in 1850, he later moved to Russell Terrace and remained in office till around 1875.

Goodhart himself was an innovator who introduced early morning communions, then a novelty in Reading. He was also a powerful preacher who, in Alfred Christopher's words, 'adorned the doctrine of God his Saviour in all things' and whose 'life was a living argument in favour of the Gospel he so faithfully preached'. Among those he reached to good effect were members of the Sutton family, first Miss Mary who after her own conversion brought her brothers, Alfred and Martin Hope Sutton, to hear the Gospel.

Martin Hope Sutton (1815-1901) had thoughts after his conversion of taking Holy Orders and entering the mission field; he was dissuaded from this course by John Ball (of St Laurence's) on the grounds that he could exercise a more effective ministry 'in the same calling wherein he was called'. That Martin was able to find his own personal vision in seedsmanship and in being a good master of men can be judged from a statement he made in 1857: 'By God's blessing we have continually prospered and increased, so that we now employ forty men and boys'. He was a Trustee of Castle Street from 1855 till his death and was involved in much good work as a Christian layman, including the restoration of Greyfriars.

In a moving letter, written a few months before his passing, Sutton excuses himself from a Trustees' Meeting: 'I cannot sit upright for many minutes together and am so very deaf that I cannot hear what is said'.

A near contemporary of his was Miss Caroline Young (1817-1902), who lived at Hare Hatch. She heard Goodhart preach while visiting friends in Reading and came to know Jesus Christ as her Saviour. Such was the affection she formed for St Mary's, Castle Street, that she eventually came to live in Reading, where she became known as a generous benefactress of the poor. She conducted Bible classes, opened a home for girls in New Town, and maintained a Scripture Reader who was located at a Mission Room on her Hare Hatch property. Miss Young bequeathed money to St Mary's, Castle Street, used partly to increase the incumbent's salary and partly to make improvements to the Chapel building through the installation of windows in the Chancel. These include her memorial window which speaks so tellingly of the central message of the Gospel, of which she was herself a faithful witness: 'We preach Christ Crucified'.

Goodhart's means, augmented by his pedagogic labours, were such that he was able to employ a curate. Rev Edward Haskins served from 1842/3 and was followed in 1845 by Charles Dent Bell (1818-98), an Irishman and graduate of Trinity College, Dublin, who subsequently ministered in Hampstead, Ambleside and Cheltenham. As well as writing a life of the pioneer missionary, Henry Martyn, and a commentary on Hebrews XI, Bell was a distinguished hymnologist. His *Church of England Hymnal* is a useful Evangelical compilation, even though it did not achieve the popularity of Bickersteth's *Hymnal Companion*. Now totally forgotten, some of his original compositions collected in *Hymns for Church and Chamber* (1884) are worthy of revival [viii].

Bell was succeeded in 1847 by Rev Charles Hole, who remained for seven years, staying on under Tubbs. Hole, who later became Rector of Loxbear in Devon and also Lecturer in Ecclesiastical History at King's College, London, is chiefly remembered as the biographer of Archdeacon Phelps, Hulme's successor at Trinity Chapel, to whose vision we owe the restoration of Greyfriars. That Hole was also possessed of a shrewd mind and a good grasp of child psychology can be seen from his advice given to a Sunday School Teachers' Meeting that 'corporal punishment ought not to be inflicted before the whole school as it was apt to make the boys try to receive it with firmness and boldness'.

Goodhart was an avid student of Eschatology, taking a firmly Premillenial line. Contending that the conversion of the Jews to faith in their true Messiah and their restoration to their own land would precede the Lord's Return, he took part in a number of symposia on such subjects, including those organised by Rev Henry Villiers, later Bishop of Durham.

These interests also led Goodhart to become a keen supporter of the London Society for the Promotion of Christianity among the Jews (now known by the less cumbersome title of the Church's Ministry among the Jews). After his removal from Reading in May 1852 to become incumbent of Park Chapel, Chelsea, he was appointed Clerical Secretary of this Society. He served from 1853 to 1868, when he resigned on taking up the living of Wetherden in Suffolk. Even thereafter he remained an Honorary Secretary of the Society and was an avid promoter of its work until his death.

Speaking of Goodhart's period of office, its historian writes that the double duties of pastoral work and missionary administration were not then 'thought beyond the power of one man to discharge, as they most certainly are at the present day. But Goodhart was no ordinary man — he dominated the Committee and ruled the missionaries with a rod of iron. Yet they all appeared to like it! For he not only thus magnified his office, but also made it honourable . . . Goodhart was the Society and the Society for the time being was Goodhart'. The same writer pays tribute to his 'ardent zeal for the cause, a rare and extensive knowledge of the subject, a wonderful business aptitude, and a burning eloquence in pulpit and platform'. And this is the man who had felt himself unfit to take up the duties at Castle Street!

Goodhart continued to show an interest in his old friends in Reading, and it is recorded that in 1890, two years prior to his death, he preached at Castle Street for the Society on the 'Connection of Jew and Gentile Salvation', with Romans IX as his text.

Let the last word on Goodhart be from a giant of a previous generation, with whom he had formed a close friendship; William Marsh described him quite simply as 'one of the noblest witnesses for God and His truth in our country'.

Charles Goodhart, Minister 1836-52.

George Ibberson Tubbs, the Chapel's longest-serving Minister, 1852-88.

GEORGE IBBERSON TUBBS 1852-1888

If James Sherman, among Ministers of Castle Street, achieved the most national renown, it is surely Goodhart's successor who is best-remembered locally. Only a few years ago, a newcomer to Reading, happening to mention to the local butcher that she worshipped at St Mary's, Castle Street, was surprised to receive the reply. 'Ah yes, Tubbses'! The 36 years in office of George Ibberson Tubbs have never been equalled and it is doubtful if they ever will. The extent to which the term 'Tubb's Chapel' or 'Tubb's' had gained acceptance can be gauged from the following story recorded by James Consterdine:

'I was once asked to take the funeral of one who belonged to a family hitherto unkown to me. Calling on the relative in charge who wished the first part of the Service to be conducted in our Church, I explained that I would have everything ready at the time fixed, at St Mary's Episcopal Chapel. With a look of anxious perplexity, as though discovering a grave mistake, he replied, "Beg pardon Sir, but I thought it was Tubb's". To a large number of people the shorter designation is by far the more familiar, if it be not the only one by which the Church is known to them.'

Prior to his ordination to the Church of England diaconate in 1847, George Tubbs had been for nine years Minister of the Independent Chapel at Warminster, Wilts, having trained for the Congregational ministry at Highbury College. In 1839, at the age of 27, he had married Ellen Hopkinson in Chorlton, Lancs, and by the time he received his licence from Bishop 'Soapy Sam' Wilberforce of Oxford and commenced his ministry in Reading on 20 June 1852, the Tubbses had a son and two daughters, another son having died in infancy. Tubbs' first years in the Anglican ministry are somewhat obscure but for the sixteen months immediately preceding his appointment to Castle Street he had been Curate of Holy Trinity, Newington, in what is now the London Borough of Soutwark.

George and Ellen Tubbs were quite a pair of rolling stones during their long residence in Reading, living at various times in Coley Place; Downshire Road (now part of Tilehurst Road); Parkside Lodge, Southern Hill (Redlands); and Mansefield, Coley Avenue. They were blessed by the addition of two further sons to their family after their move.

Tubbs was especially noted for his long sermons. Another anecdote that Consterdine clearly relished concerned a visiting preacher of a less loquacious tendency. Descending from the pulpit after half an hour or so, he was puzzled, as he made his way to the vestry, to notice many of the congregation remaining in their seats and asked one of the chapel officers if anything further was expected of him. 'No,' came the reply, 'they are waiting for their carriages, and they will have another half-hour to wait'.

Unlike other Castle Street Ministers, Tubbs does not seem to have published his homilies but a manuscript book has survived containing a series of precis of his sermons, together with those of his long-serving curate, G. Gordon Smyth. These were possibly made by a young person, perhaps a confirmand, as an exercise, for they include occasional corrections and comments in another hand. One of these summaries is reproduced here to provide a taste of a typical Tubbs sermon.

'SERMON
Preached by the Rev G I Tubbs
6th Sunday after Trinity (1874)
Text
Phil. 1. 9-11.

And this I pray, that your love may abound yet more and more in knowledge and in all judgement; That ye may approve things that are excellent; that ye may be sincere and without offence till the day of Christ; Being filled with the fruits of righteousness, which are by Jesus Christ, unto the glory and praise of God.

St Paul offered this comprehensive prayer, for the comfort of suffering fellow-workers; he assured them that the good work which was begun would continue and only be completed when both Jew and Gentile should meet in heaven. People seem to imagine that if they are loved and accepted they need nothing more, but this passage of scripture shows the greatness of their error. The child of Christ is (1st) born again, (2nd) becomes a member of Christ, a branch of the parent stem, a stone built up in Christ's temple, but he must not forget that the branch needs pruning, the stone polishing, before it is fit for heaven.

If we look at the text we shall see St Paul prays first for their love. Thus it is with the Christian; the first element he should cultivate is love. St Paul knew that the love which enters the heart of a Christian is full and deep. "We love Him because He first loved us."

It is also a well-known fact that the early Christians were ready if need be to lay down their life for Him "who gave Himself a ransom for many."

The next thing St Paul asked for was knowledge. So must a Christian grow in knowledge as well as love. There are two sorts of knowledge in which we may grow. The knowledge of Good and the knowledge of evil. Knowledge without the love of God is, St Paul says, "knowledge false before God."

Thirdly, our Text says "in all judgement". If we would be thorough sincere Christians, we must have something beside love and knowledge. Therefore the Apostle says "And this I pray that your love may abound yet more and more in knowledge *and in all judgement.*" These are the inward springs of holiness.

Let us next remark the effects of these springs. When we find a man who has been brought to God through much trial and whose life has been rough and thorny and full of trouble; that man would not be unsettled in his religion. He knows what is essential to his religion, when to stand and when to yield; knows what belongs to the world and what to God. We all ought to pray for a sagacious, discerning spirit to resist the temptation to discover "the snake in the grass".

Fourthly, we should pray to be sincere. Sincerity is one of those graces that makes little show but lies all the deeper. We should strive to keep our conscience clear, pure and unspotted from the world until the day of Christ, for we shall all need clear consciences then.

Fifthly, let us remark — the visible and abiding effects of these inward springs of holiness. When we see a man, sober, diligent, honest, we expect to find that he draws his daily light from God. The Bible says "a tree is known by its fruits". The Lord grant that we may be found fruitful unto all good works, that we may glorify his name and "be Christ's faithful soldier and servant unto our life's end."'

Tubbs contributed a chapter describing 'St Mary's Episcopal Chapel' to Ditchfield's *Ecclesiastical History of Reading*' published in 1883 and from this the pattern of services towards the end of his ministry can be seen:

'DIVINE SERVICE. Sundays, 11 a.m. and 6.30 p.m. Quarterly (for Children), 3 p.m. Wednesday, 7.30 p.m. *Holy Communion.* — First Sunday in month, after Morning Service; Second Sunday, 8 a.m.; Third Sunday, after Evening Service. *After Service.* — Every Sunday

Evening, lasting half-an-hour, in the Boys' Schoolroom, the Third Sunday excepted. *Children's Service.* — In the Boy's [sic] Schoolroom, conducted by Mr J. H. Millard and Teachers, Sundays, 11 a.m.'

One ordinance not available at the Episcopal Chapel was that of matrimony but, when need arose, Tubbs made arrangements to marry his congregation and their families at other churches in the town. Thus the marriage registers of St Mary the Virgin for 1866 to 1871 include fourteen marriages solemnized either by Tubbs or Gordon Smyth, some of which are listed below. The bridegrooms include James Freeman, Organist and Choirmaster of the Chapel, George Philbrick, a long-serving Warden and Trustee, and James Millard, the Boys' Sunday School Superintendent, mentioned above.

Date	Husband	Wife
28.8.66	James Freeman, Organist, 22 of 32 Zinzan Street	Ellen Pope, 22 of 148 Castle Street
30;.4.67	William Pratt, Tea Dealer, 30 of Hanover Square, Middlesex	Mary Ann Strong, 30 of Zinzan Place
19.11.67	Thomas Norris, Grocer, 23 of Wallingford	Emma Potts, 25 of Belle Vue Lodge
7.1.69	George Philbrick, Tanner, 27 of Katesgrove	Catherine Louisa Welch, 24 of Marlborough House
9.2.69	William George Flanagan, Veterinary Surgeon 25, of 39 Oxford Road	Isabella Wheatley (Vet's daughter) of St Mary's Butts
16.2.69	Charles Henry Biggs, School-Master, 24 of 2 Alexandra Terrace	Sarah Wiltshire, 21 of 74 Weldale Street
20.9.70	Henry Ponting, Draper, 26 of Wallingford	Kate Cundell, 24 of Oxford Road
12.4.71	George Johnson Taylor, Picture-frame Manufacturer, 27, of 43 Howard Street	Harriet Ann Clark, 25 of 14 Coley Hill
4.7.71	James Henry Millard, Managing Clerk, 26 of Russell Terrace	Sarah Strong, 23 of Zinzan Place
24.10.71	George Hobbs, Dealer, 24 of Bisham	Emily Rebecca Chalk, Widow, 28 of Grenville Terrace

An important new sphere of work for St Mary's, Castle Street commenced with Tubbs' appintment as Chaplain to the new Union Workhouse which was opened in 1867. Hitherto, each of the historic parishes of Reading had had its own workhouse and Castle Street had provided the chaplaincy for the St Mary's Poor House, which was located in Coley.

Though these were more enlightened institutions than those with which we are familiar from the pages of Dickens, the new Union Workhouse was designed to enhance the humane treatment of the inmates and at the same time to preserve their self-respect by giving them useful work to do. It was on a new site to the west of the Town Centre, in what were then reckoned to be salubrious surroundings; part of the complex still survives as Battle Hospital. This novel institution had its critics, including John Jones, writing in 1870:
'Two hundred and twenty inmates now occupy the Workhouse, and the average weekly cost for their food and clothing is 4s 7¾d. This expenditure must be regarded as bordering on extravagance, seeing that many working men who contribute to the rates do not earn enough to spend more than half that sum, per head, upon their families.'

As well as the Chaplain, the Scripture Reader and other church workers were able to minister to the spiritual needs of these poor people. The extra salary that accrued also enabled Tubbs to resume the practice of appointing curates, which had ceased after the brief curacy of C. Sterling in the mid-fifties. From 1865 till 1888, there was an unbroken line of assistants in the ordained ministry, commencing with Robert Towers, subsequently Vicar of a Kensington parish. Gordon Smyth was Curate for twelve years and later Rector of Bright, Downpatrick. He was followed in rapid succession by Sydenham Dixon, previously Curate of Greyfriars; James Hussey, who married into the Hewett family and later held rural livings in Dorset; Sholto John Henry Newman, for over forty years Vicar of Emmanuel, Hastings; and Robert Thomson, who covered the brief interregnum between Tubbs and Hubert Brooke and later served in Midlands parishes. Dixon's later ministry included a stint at Park Chapel, Chelsea (1888-98), following Goodhart's earlier ministry there. He was later a long-serving Trustee from 1910 till his death in 1932.

Important changes were made to the layout of the Chapel during Tubbs' ministry. Hitherto, the organ had been located in the gallery backing onto the portico, but in 1865 it was removed and what seems to have been substantially a new instrument erected in the present position on the north side of the chancel. This area had previously been in use as the Infants Sunday School. The space not taken up by the organ-chamber became the vestry and the original vestry adjoining the main Schoolroom was freed for use by the Sunday School and as a meeting room. At the same time the west gallery became available for use by the Infants during morning service and to provide seats for working-class people in the evening. Some of the Trustees, including Martin Hope Sutton, regarded the resiting of the organ as tending to High Church practice, but the Minister won the day with the support of the congregation.

Further changes included the removal of the old three-decker pulpit and its replacement by the present high and low pulpits. How many other churches, one wonders, can boast of *two* pulpits? The lower compartment of the three-decker pulpit had been the accustomed spot of 'Parson Brown', for whom a special seat near the Lectern was subsequently provided. The tiling of the aisles and chancel in 1882 was the other notable development dating from Tubbs' time.

Church Schools burgeoned in mid-nineteenth century Reading before the advent of state education in 1870. A day school attached to St Mary's, Castle Street, seems to have begun in a modest way in the 1850s; around 1860 a purpose-built schoolroom was erected on land to the rear of the Church, and this was extended in 1876 and 1882 to provide accommodation for over 300 chldren. The 1876 extensions were designed by the Reading-based architect, Joseph Morris (1836-1913) who had been baptised by Goodhart but later joined the weird sect of Agapemonites.

From 1872 onwards St Mary's Episcopal School faced competition from the new Board School in Coley which together, with the Parish Church's School in Hosier Street, was capable of meeting most local needs. By 1893, average attendance was down to 180 and in 1906 it was closed down. The building itself remained part of the landscape till its demolition in the 1950s; the site is now occupied by an electricity sub-station.

Early in the Tubbs era, a new Trust Deed was drawn up; dated 28 January 1856, this is the legal document that still guarantees the Chapel's independence of diocesan control and its conservative doctrinal postion. Its terms do not differ in substance from those of 1810, but clearly the origins of the chapel in the preaching of William Bromley Cadogan no longer needed spelling out.

The priority now was to ensure that the premises 'be used as and remain a place set apart and appropriated for Divine worship on the basis of the Doctrinal articles and to be conducted according to the form of Prayer used in the Church of England and for preaching therein the Gospel of our Lord Jesus Christ, administering the Sacrament of the Lord's Supper and expounding therein God's pure and holy word according to those sound and orthodox doctrines laid down and contained in the Articles and Homilies of the said Church.'

The Deed also provides a detailed job description for the Minster(s) of the Chapel and sets out the arrangements to be followed in the event of dissatisfaction with the conduct or doctrinal position of any such Minister. It also authorises the Trustees to use money accruing from the sale of the Chapel 'in or towards the support of any other Chapel which may then be standing within the Town of Reading . . . or its vicinity and may be carried on upon the same footing as the said chapel', with the London Missionary Society, as before, benefiting 'in default thereof'.

The original Trustees had by now gone to their rest but for the most part their successors represented a similar cross-section of the community. Although there was now one clergyman, Rev Henry John Neale Chase, of Bridge near Canterbury, the Trustees were still chiefly composed of local laymen. The medical profession remained in strength, with Charles Cowan, Doctor of Medicine, who practised in London Street, John Woodroffe Workman, surgeon, who had been a partner of Thomas Ring, Charles May anbd Robert Parsons Miller, each a chemist and druggist. James Trendell, Thomas Lawrance and Joseph Whatley represented the gentry; and George Dunlop carried on the traditional links with the drapery trade. Of Martin Hope Sutton, seedsman, we have already made mention. Finally, in the tradition of Mr 'Bottle' Tanner, there were two brewers, Thomas Hawkins, now the leading light of the Castle Brewery, and Robert Hewett, whose Victoria Brewery was located in Chain Street.

Both these men were notable benefactors. Hawkins, forty years a Trustee till his death in 1894, had owned the land on which part of the School buildings was built and also contributed a sum of £1,000 to provide income for augmenting the stipend and supplementing church finances. Of Robert Hewett (1811-1904) one can do no better than quote James Consterdine's obituary in the *Monthly Magazine*.

'His connexion with our congregation was one of very long standing, for when a boy at Barkham, together with his mother, he from time to time visited the church in the days of James Sherman. For a considerable number of years he has been chairman of our Trustees, and also held the office of Churchwarden, besides being the largest contributor to the various charities and funds belonging to St Mary's Chapel, His gifts were marked by an absence of display and by a kindliness which made them doubly valuable. An earnest believer in the power of prayer, he was large-hearted and of wide sympathy, and withal thoroughly staunch and loyal to the simple Gospel of Jesus Christ.'

Like the Castle Brewery, Hewett's Victoria Brewery was swallowed up into the Simonds empire early in the 20th century. James Dymore Brown, celebrated for his Family Pale Ale, supplied to the Royal Berkshire Hospital, who had also been a sidesman and a Trustee, had already severed his connections with the Chapel in 1902. The beerage's connection with the chapel thus died out with the Hewetts' withdrawal from brewing.

Other prominent laymen of the Tubbs era included two of a family of French Huguenot descent: Colonel Charles Young Bazett, a retired Indian Army officer, and his brother, Mr Richard Young Bazett, sometimes referred to as Judge Bazett, who conducted a Men's Bible Class and acted as Secretary of the Reading Church Missionary Association. They occupied, though not simultaneously, two houses of some substance on the Bath Road, Springfield and Highfield. Four of Mr Bazett's daughters were called to overseas mission fields. The high esteem in which Tubbs himself must have held the Bazett family can be seen in the choice of the name Cyril Bazett for his third son, born in 1858.

It was Colonel Bazett who had the sorrowful task of conveying the congregation's sympathy to Mr and Mrs Tubbs on the death of their eldest son, Charles, and daughter, Mary, who both died during a cholera outbreak in India in 1865. The memorial erected in the chancel as an expression of this sympathy is the earliest of the four memorials to be found in the Chapel.

The esteem with which Tubbs was held can be seen not only from this touching gesture but also from the presentation of a silver bowl and cheque for £460 to mark his Silver Jubilee as Minister and the even more generous parting gift of 1,000 guineas, which was intended in lieu of a pension and which coincided with his golden wedding in 1888.

Just before the Minister's retirement focussed their attention, the Trustees found themselves dealing with a bizarre series of complaints from one of the Butts shopkeepers. Mr Thompson, whose butcher's shop backed on to the church school, alleged that sewage from this source was seeping into his bacon store. His customers, it transpired, were not at all impressed by this novel method of curing their ham. The legal ramifications perplexed the Trustees over several meetings and diagrams of the offending drains were solemnly reproduced in the Minutes.

Tubbs' retirement was hastened by a serious illness. On 25 October 1888, he announced his decision in a letter to his 'beloved friends', which includes the following exhortation:
'Those of you, who have believed and accepted the Gospel in our dear old Church, owe to her a debt of grateful interest. Let me beseech you to be true to her; don't lightly forsake her, thinking you are quite released, because the old Pastor is gone . . .
'Many of you I held at the Baptismal font; many I prepared for the solemn rite of Confirmation; and many others have told me that I have been used for their edification and comfort. Your names are written on my heart, so I earnestly beseech you to hold fast to the form of sound words — hear only a full Gospel'.

Tubbs' last Sunday, 16 December, which coincided with the 90th anniversary of the Chapel, was another of the great occasions in the life of St Mary's, Castle Street. The Church was full to overflowing, with the shutters between the chancel and the upper Schoolroom having to be removed to accommodate those unable to find a seat in the nave and galleries. Tubbs appropriately took his text from Paul's parting words to the elders of Ephesus in Acts 20. Some words from this sermon conclude our account of his ministry:
'Worthy friends may be taken from you, faithful ministers may be removed, but the Lord Jesus Christ remains unchangeable, the same, full of power, full of love, full of blessings . . .
'My aim has been to urge upon you the simplicity and fullness of the Gospel of Christ, that by God's grace each of you might be enabled truly to say "the life which I now live I live by faith in the Son of God, who loved me and gave Himself for me." [Gal.2.20] And now, in my parting address, I have no other doctrine to bring before you. My last words shall be to hold up with both hands a crucified, risen, living, coming Christ . . .'

George and Ellen Tubbs retired to Boscombe and for some years entertained the Castle Street Sunday School Annual Outing to Bournemouth. In 1892, Tubbs was fit enough to walk with them to the station to see them off, but on 3 May 1893 his long and fruitful life came to a close. Ellen survived him by seven years.

The High Pulpit installed during Tubbs' time.

When Baptized.	Child's Christian Name.	Parents' Names.		Abode.	Quality, Trade, or Profession.	By whom the Ceremony was performed.
		Christian.	Surname.			
1891 June 28th No. 281	Frederick Robert Born May 3. 1891	Robert & Eliza	Hitchman	94 Elgar Road Katesgrove	Carpenter	A.S. Weatherhead
1891 June 28th No. 282	Phyllis Absalom Born May 10th 1891.	James Joseph & Mary Elizabeth	Ross	11 Hosier Street	Labourer	A.S. Weatherhead
1891 June 2nd No. 283	Ebenezer		Harding	28 Dover Street	Potter	A.S. Weatherhead
1891 July 14th No. 284	Blandy Born May 17	Walter & Ellen	Parsons	Castle Crescent	Corn Merchant	David Wood
1891 July 17th No. 285	Sylvia Hazel Born: Oct 29th 1890	Thomas & Frances Ada	Cooke	Southcot Cresc	Wholesale	Hubert
1891 August 9th No. 286	Charles James August Born: March 24th 1878.	Charles George & Harriet	Oppermann	Hulme Villa, Oxford Road		
1891 August 9th No. 287	Percival Herrman Born Dec 18 1879	Charles George & Harriet	Oppermann	Hulme Villa, Oxford Road		
1891 August 9th No. 288	Sarah Elise Born: Feb 20 1883	Charles George & Harriet	Oppermann	Hulme Villa Oxford Road		

Extract from the Chapel's Baptismal Register, recording the adult baptism of Ebenezer Harding. INSET: Hubert Brooke, Minister 1888-95.

INTO ALL THE WORLD 1888-1895

The man chosen to succeed George Ibberson Tubbs was no stranger to Berkshire. Hubert Brooke MA (Cantab) had served for two years as Curate of St Mary Magdalene, Maidenhead, following his ordination by the Bishop of Oxford in 1875. Meanwhile he had been Perpetual Curate of St Bride's, Liverpool from 1878 to 1885 and had also (from 1883) become closely associated with the work of the Keswick Convention.

During the years following its foundation in 1875, Keswick had come under considerable suspicion from such Evangelical leaders as Brooke's Bishop, J. C. Ryle of Liverpool; to them its particular view of personal holiness, which stressed the importance of victory over every known sin, was seen as verging towards a dangerous perfectionism prevalent on the Continent, which taught that the true Christian was incapable of sin. Brooke and others like him helped to allay such fears, by broadening the scope of the Convention and by inspiring the movement's followers with a missionary vision that took them beyond narrow personal pietism. He was a signatory of the 'Keswick letter' of 1890 by which the Convention leaders and CMS representatives jointly drew the attention of the Church at large to the tremendous need for missionaries in the field, especially in India, China and among the 'recently-discovered' African tribes.

Brooke's missionary interests were not motivated solely by a hunger for souls. In Consterdine's words, 'he spoke very plainly of the duty and privilege of personal consecration and whole-hearted surrender to God, and he insisted that such consecration should be evidenced by obedience to our Lord's parting command to be His witnesses to all nations'. Just as Goodhart had seen the conversion of the Jews as an essential step in the process leading to the return of the Lord Jesus Christ, so Hubert Brooke took seriously the Lord's words: 'This Gospel of the Kingdom shall be preached in all the world for a witness unto all nations; *and then shall the end come*' (Matt. 24.5) By 1911 he had become convinced that the Lord's return was indeed imminent. In *The Fact and Features of the Lord's Return* he writes:

'Look at the last 120 years, beginning with the French Revolution, and see how one nation after another has suffered from revolutionary and anarchic outbreaks. . . . What do these things mean? . . . Are these not times when in nation after nation "the sun is being darkened and the moon losing her light, and the powers of heaven being shaken"?'

Eighty years and several great dictators later, we may still not have reached the moment of the Second Coming, but we would do well to heed Brooke's advice, to watch for the signs and to continue to attempt to fulfill the Lord's Great Commission.

Before Brooke's ministry, St Mary's, Castle Street had regarded Reading as its principal sphere of activity. There are no records of any workers sent into the foreign field before 1888, apart from John Ross, one of Sherman's acolytes, in the 1830s. There was, however, a potent example before the congregation in the person of Thomas Valpy French, a man described by the CMS historian, Eugene Stock, as 'the most distinguished of all CMS missionaries.'

As Stephen Neill has said, 'in him zeal was not always matched with prudence, but it is fortunate for the Church that its greatest men are not always prudent. In his old age French decided on an apparently reckless and hopeless venture'. He was determined to go into Muscat in Arabia and to attempt to evangelise the Islamic World at its very heart; he arrived there on 8 February 1891 but by 14 May he was dead.

Archdeacon Moule was moved to verse:

> 'Where Muscat fronts the Orient Sun
> 'Twixt heaving sea and rocky steep,
> His work of mercy scarce begun,
> A saintly soul has fallen asleep:
> Who comes to lift the Cross instead?
> Who takes the standard from the dead?

In Reading, that same year, the Cross was taken up by James Redman and Thomas Simmonds and within ten years St Mary's, Castle Street, had twenty-four missionaries serving overseas.

From the pages of the Chapel's *Monthly Magazine* for 1891, it is possible to deduce a mounting excitement. In March, Brooke writes to remind his readers of the need to 'awaken the living Church to the real Call of Christ to Missionary work'. In May, the month when a deputation speaker from CMS was preaching in the Chapel, the subscribers were to read that 'one of our congregation, Mr J. H. Redman, has now been accepted by the CMS; and will be leaving before the end of the Autumn for work abroad'. It was suggested to them that, in order to support, as well as send, their own missionary, they might consider subscribing a penny a day, which from 70 or 80 people, amounting to £105/120 per annum, 'would probably suffice for all the necessary expenses of a single missionary, when once in the field'. Giving to CMS that month amounted to nearly £57, of which about half came from a single source; previously it had averaged £70 per annum. By the time he was writing the July letter, Brooke was able to announce that £126 had been pledged to support 'Our Own Missionary'.

The following month, he could add that two more recruits had come forward, the two Misses Bazett having been accepted for service in Mombasa after completing the CMS training course. They might well have gone out earlier, except that their father (who died in 1889) had been reluctant to let his young daughters risk their lives in the Dark Continent! It was, however, another man, Thomas Simmonds, who pipped both James Redman and the Misses Bazett at the post for the privilege of being the first to depart. He left for the Szechuen region of China on 31 October, while Redman sailed for East Africa on 23 November, in a party led by the Bishop of Uganda, Alfred Robert Tucker.

Like French in Arabia, Redman was destined to be a torchbearer for others rather than a winner of souls. He reached East Africa in time to spend Christmas with his fellow-missionaries and by the end of January he was able to report that he had been 'appointed to labour at Mamboia, in the German sphere of East African territory' (now Tanzania). By that time, he had the 'experience of nursing a sick fellow-labourer' and had himself already suffered a short bout of fever. After setting off from Zanzibar on 28 February, to cross to the mainland, he landed at Saadani, a place noted for its unsalubriousness, and so passed on quickly to Ndumi. But there he fell sick from a severe fever and without the aid of a doctor died the following day.

The sad loss of James Redman did not discourage the people of St Mary's, Castle Street. Rather did his sacrifice fire others to follow him and those not called to go where inspired to give. The Own Missionary Fund was for a time renamed the Redman Fund and contributions continued to pour in. The amount given to overseas missions rose to £500 per annum and in 1899, another great year of sending, reached a remarkable £836.

The news of Thomas Simmonds was rather happier and by 1895 the YMCA, for whom he worked, was able to tell the congregation at Castle Street that 'when you sent us Mr Simmonds, you sent us a good missionary'.

The three Bazett sisters, Louisa, Mary and Sibella, finally sailed out to East Africa together on 24 October 1892. It is recorded that 1,100 were present at a valedictory meeting for them and a Greyfriars missionary, held at the Assembly Rooms. In 1893, Louisa, generally called Louie, married Mr J. R. W. Pigott, the administrator of the British East Africa Company, a godly man who gave much practical assistance to the CMS missionaires. Mary (1866-1948) was forced to return home in 1895 through ill-health but in 1899 she married Rev (later Canon) Harry Leakey (1868-1940) who had originally come to Reading in 1884 to teach French at the Grammar School. They returned to Kenya in 1901 and devoted all their lives to the country, latterly based at Limuru near Narobi. Their children included Louis (1903-72), the renowned anthropologist and Julia, who married Rev (later Bishop) Lawrence Barham, a pioneer missionary in Rwanda.

In 1902, Sibella (1868-1954), who had been Superintendent of the Infants' Sunday School before her call to mission, married Rev George Burns (1869-1944). He had been in Nairobi since 1892 in government service but entered the mission field in 1898, under the New South Wales Association of CMS. He later ministered at Shimba, becoming Archdeacon of Mombasa in 1935. Like the Leakeys, the Burns lived out their days in Kenya.

Two other members of this remarkable family became missionaries by marriage. In 1898. Ellen Bazett (1860-1953), married Rev Edward Cyril Gordon (1858-1926), a relative of the martyred Bishop Hannington, who had travelled with him on his 1882 expedition. The Gordons returned to England in 1902 and Edward Gordon was placed on the disabled list in 1905. He translated Mark, Luke and Acts into Lugandan. Finally, in 1899, Mabel Gertrude Bazett (d1936) married Richard Herbert Leakey (1868-1937), a first cousin once-removed of Harry, from Blaby, Leicestershire, who had been working in Uganda since 1892. Richard Leakey was ordained in 1901 and made a Canon of Mengo Cathedral in 1917. He and Mabel returned to England in 1924, latterly living at Exmouth. Canon Ian Leakey, the present Chairman of Mid-Africa Ministry, belongs to this branch of the Leakeys.

Another distinguished missionary associated with Castle Street was Richard J. Hunt, who was sent out by the South American Missionary Society in 1894 to work among the Chaco Indians of Argentina. Hunt, who also worked in Paraguay, was a pioneer-translator of the Scriptures into the languages of the South American Indians and was called 'the Livingstone of South America' by his biographer.

The last of the missionaries of note sent out from Castle Street is the Ven Ernest Scudamore Tanner (1874-1960). Tanner came from Lewisham but was educated in Reading and worked as a jeweller. He went out to India in 1898, under CMS, initially labouring among the Telegu people in Ellore and was supported by SMCS as 'Our Own Missionary'. In 1902 he married Mary Louisa White (d1942) and was also ordained priest by the Bishop of Madras. He later served in Masulipatam, Rhagavapuram and Bezwada, and from 1931 till his retirement in 1938 as Archdeacon of Kistna. (Other missionaries sent out from Castle Street then are listed in Appendix Two).

Hubert Brooke attracted like-minded men as his curates. Two young men, Arthur Swinton Weatherhead (1889-93) and Harrington Clare Lees (1893-95), served their first curacies under him and both suffered the disappointment of being rejected for service with CMS on health grounds. Weatherhead, the son of a missionary in Bombay, went on to conventional parochial ministry, including lengthy pastorates in Hereford, Huddersfield and Norwich. Lees later became Vicar of Christ Church, Beckenham, and from 1910 one of the Castle Street Trustees. He resigned this office in 1921 on his appointment as Archbishop of Melbourne. During home-leave in 1928, the year before his death, he came to Reading with his wife to open the Chapel's fête which, because of inclement weather, was held in All Saints' Hall rather than its usual location in the grounds of the Hewetts' nearby house. The late Phyllis Adams recalled how this rather portly, bow-legged gentleman, dressed in a three-quarter-length coat and black silk top-hat, posed for a photograph, looking as if he had stepped straight out of the pages of Trollope!

In spite of the commendable enthusiasm Brooke aroused for overseas missions, the home front was not neglected during his ministry. Since the days of Parson Brown, the offices of Chapel Clerk and Scripture Reader had been separated, with Mr J. C. Falla, residing in the Chapel House, carrying out the former duties, whereas the latter were the responsibility of George Holloway. His tenth annual report for 1890/91 shows that during the year he chalked up 1,316 general visits, 908 visits to the sick, 49 men's Bible classes, 152 Cottage and Schoolroom meetings and 70 open air services. 'The Cottage Meetings during the Winter, and Open Air services in the Summer months, have also been regularly held. Cordial welcome is generally given, with a very rare objection or repulse; and by the hearty assistance of the good band of voluntary workers, the number both of in-door and out-door Meetings is considerably larger than in former days'. When Mr Holloway, who latterly lived in Sherman Road, died in 1900 at the age of 64, he was described by James Consterdine as 'a soul-winner much blessed of God'. The Trustees showed their gratitude by providing financial support to his wife and children. A daughter of Mr Holloway married Richard Hunt, the missionary.

A family with a long connection with St Mary's, Castle Street first appeared on the scene in the 1890s. Its founder was Ebenezer Harding a countryman from Checkendon, born in 1856, who came to Reading to work as a potter at E. & S. Collier's. His mother and sisters were believers and had, it seems, prayed for him for many years, but it was not until one Sunday he heard Hubert Brooke preach that he was led to Christ himself. As Ebenezer desired baptism by total immersion, he was taken by Arthur Weatherhead to the nearby Carey Baptist Church, where the sacrament was administered.

Ebenezer Harding was a man of distinguished mien, with a long white beard that made one member of the congregation liken him to one of the patriarchs of old — he lived to a correspondingly great age, dying at the age of 90. He was blessed with ten children and it is notable that two of these baptised at Castle Street during the 1890s, Mabel and Mary Sibella, received the names of three of the Bazett sisters — a further indication of the Bazett influence on all with whom they came into contact. The Hardings lived in Dover Street and later in Berkeley Avenue.

Arthur Harding worked as an insurance agent, was a Lieutenant in the Boys Brigade, and People's Warden and a Trustee for over twenty years until his death in 1947 at the age of sixty. Writing in the church magazine, Bill Appleby called him 'one of God's gentlemen' and recalled the esteem, in which he was held by 'the poorer people of the town'. All 'looked forward to seeing 'Mr Harding'; so much so, that his working hours were often prolonged, since he *must* stop and admire this youngster, or that piece of furniture'. Arthur Harding and his wife, Jessie, were among the first couples to be married in St Mary's, Castle Street after the Chapel was granted a licence in 1914; the new communion rails in the nave were given in their memory.

Alice Harding (1884-1979), who became Mrs Adams, was a lady of considerable literary talent and with the ability to recall the events of her childhood with great clarity. She could recollect 'being held up in someone's arms' at the age of three 'outside Tubbses Church one night when Simonds was on fire and a door in the road opposite opened so that we could see across the space behond'. At the age of twelve she won a Certificate of Merit from the Band of Hope for excellence in reporting a lecture on 'Alcohol and the Human Body' and in adult life she continued her literary pursuits, especially her poetry. Her 'Anniversary

Hymn' is well known to members of the congregation, but an extract from a Christmas carol, written in December 1946, may be of more general interest, particularly as it treats the Mother and Child theme with reverence but without falling into Roman Catholic errors of undue devotion to Mary:

> 'Mother, with the Babe Divine
> Cradled in that warm embrace,
> What sweet, precious thoughts are thine
> As thou lookest on his face?
> This dear baby Jesus,
> Thy dear baby Jesus . . .
>
> 'Fold him closely to thy breast,
> Softly, sweetly to him sing,
> There in slumber let him rest;
> This thy Prophet, Priest and King,
> This dear baby Jesus.
> THIS THY SAVIOUR JESUS.'

The Harding family connection with St Mary's, Castle Street, has continued to the present: Mrs Adams' daughter, Phyllis, was a member of the church until her death in 1991 and Arthur Harding's daughter, Barbara, who is married to Rev John Hurst, is one of the Trustees.

Hubert Brooke suffered a breakdown in health late in 1894, a bout of influenza causing severe strain on the heart. His doctors advised him against spending another winter in the damp Thames Valley climate. After two years as winter Chaplain at Les Avants, Switzerland, he accepted the incumbency of St Margaret's in Brighton. He continued to be an important force in CMS and at the Keswick Convention, where his expository Bible readings were particularly admired. He was a speaker at the CMS Centenary in 1899, when his theme typically was World Evangelisation.

Eventually, even the duties at more salubrious Brighton became too much for Brooke's health but, on his retirement in 1910, he took on a new role as a Missioner-cum-Travelling Secretary for CMS who considered that he 'of all living clergymen is perhaps the most entirely qualified to set forth Missions as pre-eminently the work of the Lord' and 'to expound their Scriptural basis and principles'. The keen interest he retained in St Mary's, Castle Street is indicated by his frequent visits to its pulpit and his service as a Trustee from 1910 till his death in 1930.

St Mary's Choir, with Rev Hubert Brooke in 1893. The young Arthur
Harding is second on the right in the middle row.

A New Century Dawns 1895-1915

'It will be my aim with God's help to preach no new doctrine, but the same Gospel you have always heard preached in the pulpit of St Mary's Chapel, that Gospel which is yet as much as it was in St Paul's day, "The power of God unto salvation". May I ask your earnest prayers to God for a blessing on our work together for His glory? Pray that we all may be made and kept like our dear Master and brought very close to Him. Pray too that the Missionary spirit, which I rejoice to hear exists so largely amongst you, may be maintained and strengthened, and that the offerings of both money and of personal service for this blessed work, so dear to the heart of our Saviour, may never cease; also that as a congregation we may in our own souls and in our labour for Christ at home reap abundantly the benefit which always comes to those who obey our Lord's parting command, "Go teach all nations".'

Thus did the man chosen to succeed Hubert Brooke introduce himself to his flock. James Consterdine was of the same generation as his predecessor, having been ordained the year after Brooke. His father, James Whitworth Consterdine, had held livings at Chorley and Alderley Edge and, as a boy, James the younger had attended Manchester Grammar School. He took honours in History at Lincoln College, Oxford, and was then curate of Christ Church, Westminster from 1876-1882. After his marriage the following year, he worked as an Army Chaplain at Peshawar in the Punjab for fourteen months, an experience that may have helped him to share Hubert Brooke's missionary concerns. After his return he was incumbent of St John's, Ashbourne, in Derbyshire for six years. Before coming to Reading he was first Curate and then Vicar of Little Heath, now part of Potters Bar in Hertfordshire, and also held at the same time the South-East Secretaryship of the Church Pastoral Aid Society (CPAS). He commenced his twenty-year cure of souls in Reading in November 1895 at the age of 43.

During Mr Consterdine's ministry important changes were made to the structure of the building and to the conduct of Sunday services. Just as the Chapel's Silver Jubilee had been marked by the transition from candlelight to gas, so the centenary in 1898 was celebrated by the installation of electric lighting. The considerable discomfort experienced by members of the congregation from heat generated by the gas-lamps during the summer influenced the change. The Trustees formed a Committee to examine the cost and determine the most suitable method of lighting. This consisted of Colonel Bazett junior, Mr Falla, the Clerk, Thomas Hewett, son of Robert and Mr Warrick, who manufactured Monarch bicycles and sold them from his shop in the Butts. After visiting the new (1894) Wesleyan chapel in Oxford Road and Hubert Brooke's church in Brighton, the Committee recommended a system similar to that used in the former, with brackets attached to the sides of the Galleries, and brackets, pendants and three-light clusters under the galleries and in the chancel. The cost of this work, carried out by Messrs Callas, was just in excess of £100 and was met by generous donations from the veteran Trustees, Robert Hewett and Martin Hope Sutton, together with the proceeds of the Centenary collections and a tea-party held in West Street Hall. The work was completed by summer 1899, and the congregation was generally pleased with the improved climatic conditions. A notebook and cigarette card dating from the time of the original installation were discovered during recent rewiring.

The alterations to the east end financed by Caroline Young's legacy left in 1902 were made at Consterdine's suggestion and motivated partly by a desire to improve the lighting of the chancel. The installation of the three windows also necessitated the removal of the Ten Commandments to their present position either side of the chancel arch. Following the completion of these works the Church was redecorated throughout with such thoroughness that no substantial changes to the decor were necessary until 1970. The text over the chancel arch, originally inscribed in Gothic lettering and in its longer form. 'Whosoever will let him take the water of life freely' (Rev. 22.17), dates from this time. A further addition was a memorial tablet to Corporal William Henry Cross, killed in 1900 during the Boer War, aged 21.

In 1905, the resourceful Mr Consterdine was at work again with a scheme to alter the Communion rails. On this occasion he did not get his way immediately and it was not until 1914 that the rails were brought into their present position in a straight line across the chancel instead of their previous location on three sides of the Lord's Table; this had been cramping for the clergy and some communicants were distracted by finding themselves face to face with each other. Earlier, in 1912, the choir stalls had been removed from the chancel and placed in the nave to accommodate a growing number of choristers and at the same time the organ received a much-needed overhaul following an inspection by Henry Willis junior.

Consterdine had further difficulties in persuading the Trustees when he wanted to make changes in pulpit vesture. It had always been the tradition at St Mary's, Castle Street, as in many other Anglican churches, to read the service in a surplice, but to change to the black Geneva preaching gown for the sermon.

By the 1890s a growing number of Evangelicals felt that the change of garment was an unnecessary distraction and that there were no doctrinal implications in wearing the surplice throughout the service. In 1901, therefore, Consterdine approached the Trustees with a request that the arrangement whereby he was required to preach in a black gown should be set aside. The Trustees were split down the middle on this question, some such as the Hewetts and Daniel Heelas supporting the Minister, while others held fast to the old tradition. These included a military contingent much to the fore at this time, comprising General McGregor and Colonels Bazett and Williams. All agreed, however, with a compromise suggested by Mr Arthur Sutton to consult the seat-holders, eighty percent of whom were in favour of the proposed alteration. Even so, the diehards stood their ground and it was not until well into 1902, following a positive vote by the congregation at the Annual Vestry Meeting and a third series of votes on the matter by the Trustees, that the Minister's wishes were finally met.

In recent years, the use of a black gown, formerly worn at St John in the Wall, Bristol, has been resumed as a witness to the primacy of the preaching of God's word at a time when so many congregations are served with a surfeit of sacramental services.

James Consterdine aroused further controversy by introducing a surpliced choir, which some saw as a Romeward move. There was no disagreement, however, when in 1912, at the age of 114, the Chapel was at last licensed for the solemnization of marriage. The licence was granted by the Bishop of Oxford and founder of the Liberal Catholic tradition in the Church of England, Charles Gore, on the grounds that 'it would relieve from inconvenience the Mother Parish of Saint Mary the Virgin, if the Proprietary Chapel of St Mary, Castle Street, situate within the said Parish were licensed for the publication of Banns and the solemnization of Marriage'. The inconvenience to members of the Castle Street congregation in having to use the Parish Church for their nuptials was clearly considered of secondary importance.

Of the Church's work among young people, there were significant developments during Mr Consterdine's incumbency. The first twenty years of the century was a time of particularly rich flowering for the Sunday Schools which then numbered some 800 to 1,000 children. Once a year, 'it was quite a sight,' in Alice Harding Adams' words, 'seeing a thousand children on the Sunday School treat in Prospect Park, marching behind the huge silk Sunday School banner with their teachers'. A police escort was needed, even in those comparatively traffic-free times.

Sunday School and Bible classes were held at ten in the morning and three in the afternoon. The success of ths ministry to young people was to a great extent due to the faithfulness and whole-hearted dedication of the teachers, who would regularly meet together to pray for the children before the classes began in the morning and after the conclusion of the afternoon school.

In the early years of the century, the Infants' School was run by Miss Flanagan, and the Girls by Miss Gill, succeeded in 1903 by Miss Hart, whose family ran an ironmongery business in Gun Street. In the Boys' School Mr Millard was followed by Mr Long, the Chapel Clerk, and Mr Warrick, the bicycle manufacturer. Later Mr Reeves took over the Boys, assisted by Mr Hinder, who was chauffeur to the Hewett family, and Mr Duffield who worked for Venners, the Berkshire bacon people. His hands were always chapped from working in brine, but in spite of his hardships he not only gave up his Sundays to teach the children but also helped his sister run open-air missions which were the means of attracting many young people to the Saviour. When Arthur Duffield died in 1929, aged 65, the Minister spoke 'very feelingly of the loss the Church has sustained' by the death of such an 'earnest and devout worker' and the Chapel Council sent a message of sympathy to his sister.

Lady teachers included Miss Holloway, who became Infants Superintendent, and the Misses Winnie and Amy Goodacre. At a slightly later date, there was a rather eccentric lady called Miss Perry, who deserved 'a crown of endurance' for faithfully teaching God's word in the face of relentless persecution from the boys of the Sunday School. She used to carry a very large watch with a face like Big Ben and the boys were continually running up to her to ask the time. She also wore a capacious hat which the boys liked to decorate by dropping pieces of paper under its turned up rim. Finally, when she had completed her class, she would find that one of the young rascals had ridden off on her bicycle, and she was obliged to give chase.

St Mary's Sunday School is still in existence, though it now only meets in the morning during the second half of the service and the days when 800 children would gather to learn God's Word are, alas, long since passed.

It was in 1903 that the 7th Reading Company of the Boys' Brigade was established at Castle Street as a branch of the Sunday School work. Although six other companies had been formed in Reading from 1901 onwards, including those at Greyfriars, St John's and Broad Street, most of these were of brief duration. The 7th Reading, however, in spite of several vicissitudes, including periods in abeyance and even outright hostility on the part of some incumbents, still survives and justly claims to be the oldest company in the Reading Battalion of the BB.

The vision of founding the Company seems to have been that of one man, the 22-year-old Arthur Minchin, who was a teacher in the Sunday School and also a 5th Year Trooper in the Berkshire Imperial Yeomanry. The company was formally enrolled on 5 November with Minchin as Captain, Charles Pope as Lieutenant and James Consterdine as Chaplain. Initially, there were 55 boys on the roll, with average attendance around 38; these figures rose to 88 and 63 the following year, but thereafter the initial enthusiasm wore off a little. One or two of the old 'buffers' in the congregation were later drafted in to help, for in 1909 we find General MacGregor of the Royal Artillery and Colonel Richard Bazett serving as President and Secretary.

Arthur Minchin resigned in 1908 and later entered the mission field. His place was taken briefly by Consterdine's Curate, Rev Charles Horace Bellamy, and on his departure William Holmes, of the celebrated furnishing company, was promoted from Lieutenant to Captain, in which office he served till 1925. Others whose long service deserves mention include William Haines, Arthur Harding, Bob Evans, Frank Westbrook, Wilfrid Newbery, Percy Frewin, Harry Frost and Bill Appleby, who became Secretary of the Reading Battalion when it was formed in 1950. The present long-serving Captain is Denis Richmond.

Towards the end of his long life of distinguished service to the extension of Christ's Kingdom in Reading, Ernest William 'Bill' Appleby (1899-1984) penned some reminiscences of the earlier days of the 7th Reading with the rather Wellsian title, *The Shape of Things to Come:*
'The year is 1910 and the month September; a small group of boys meet together in St Mary's Butts before going into the passageway between Warrick's the cycle shop and the tobacconist. As is usual with boys we were a mixed bunch; but on this occasion we all had the same objective . . . Under the direction of a boy named Leonard Hall who lived in Elgar Road we had been coerced into joining the 7th Reading Company of the Boys' Brigade, affiliated to the church around the corner . . .
'Alf' Knott, resplendent in the uniform of a sergeant . . . met us in the hall, looked us up and down but was very discreet as to his personal opinion of each of us! At the far table in the long school-room Mr William Holmes was seated. Very awe-inspiring he was, we had heard that he was a prominent business man, but even more important he had taken over the Captainship of the 7th Reading Company . . .
But perhaps even more important I met a further personality who became a part of my life . . . He was a Lieutenant in the Company, Mr Frank Westbook. He had the ability to find boys saying "Sir" when they spoke, not that he desired anything like that, but because he had something about him which was strange to us. What could that have been?'

Frank Westbrook, after a spell as Captain, was later to co-found the 99th London Company when he moved to Streatham in 1928. Though he was a loss to the 7th Reading, his move led to a happy association between the two companies which camped together for many years on the Isle of Wight.

Just as James Consterdine continued in Hubert Brooke's footsteps, by inspiring men and women to offer themselves for the mission field, so he was also able to provide practical help to some of the missionaries. When the Church acquired a new set of silver communion vessels in 1910, the old electro-plated vessels were sent to George Burns in Nairobi and Ernest Tanner in Madras. Consterdine was also able to commandeer the assistance in the ministry of recently returned missionaries. This was especially helpful at a time when St Mary's, Castle Street, as a non-parochial church, was increasingly unattractive to fresh young curates who looked for a regular parish situation as a training-ground for their future ministry. Percy Wood, who had been in Cairo, served from 1898 to 1900, J. G. B. Hollins from Palestine in 1903-4 and Francis Rowling from Uganda in 1911-12.

In 1906, Rev Harry Leakey came home on sick leave from Kenya, bringing with him not only his wife, Mary and their three children, but also a Kikuyu boy named Stefano, who had been baptised by him and who was helping him translate the Bible into the Kikuyu language. It was the first time most people in Reading had seen a native African. Stefano's visit earned Leakey a reprimand from CMS who were opposed to introducing Africans into an alien way of life. However, the boy did not seem to suffer from exposure to either the culture or the climate of Reading; his assistance with the translation was invaluable and he went on to become interpreter to the High Court in Nairobi.

Towards the end of his ministry in Reading, James Consterdine lost his wife, Susanna, who died in 1913 aged 54. The manner of his leaving Castle Street was rather unusual. On 5 May 1915, he wrote to the Trustees to inform them that the Rector of Edgware, 'the Revd Hubert Phelps, who is 84 or 85 and very ill,' had asked him to be his successor. Phelps had secured the patronage of the living and placed it in the hands of his wife. Consterdine told the Trustees that he expected to leave Reading by the end of the year but was unable to give a definite date until the Edgware living could be formally offered to him.

This put the Trustees in an awkward position, since they did not feel able to begin the search for a new incumbent until a definite date was known. In the event, the problem was resolved by the early death of Phelps in June 1915. Consterdine remained formally in charge at Castle Street till the end of September, ministering for the last time on the 26th, but in the meantime also took some services in his new parish.

James Consterdine retained an interest in his old friends in Reading and made occasional visits to the pulpit at Castle Street. He remained at Edgware until his death, which occurred on 14 August 1925 while he was visiting his brother, Reginald, then Vicar of Lindow in Derbyshire. He was buried four days later and a commemoration service was held at Castle Street on the 23rd. On this occasion, Sydney Skeens, who had been recommended for the incumbency by Consterdine, preached on the text from the parable of the wise and foolish virgins in Matthew 25, 'They that were ready went in'.

We may conclude this account by quoting from a letter Consterdine sent to the Trustees in 1922, wishing God's blessing on the ministry of Sydney Skeens, who was, he said, to be 'congratulated on coming to minister to a congregation from which I received so many personal kindnesses during the twenty years in which I held the Incumbency, not the least being the sympathy and consideration shown in the illness and loss of my dear wife.

'I shall constantly pray that God's blessing may rest on my old flock and on my brother's ministry among you.'

ABOVE: St Mary's Butts with Warrick's cycle shop at extreme left.
(BLAT) BELOW: Castle Street early in the 20th century (BLAT)
OPPOSITE LEFT: James Consterdine, Minister 1895-1915. RIGHT:
The Ten Commandments as repositioned during Mr Consterdine's
ministry. (ES) BELOW: The unveiling of a framed photograph of Canon
Minchin, founder of the 7th Reading Company of the Boys Brigade.

79

1914. Marriage solemnized at St Mary's Castle Street, Reading in the Parish of St Mary's in the County of Berkshire

No.	When Married.	Name and Surname.	Age.	Condition.	Rank or Profession.	Residence at the time of Marriage.	Father's Name and Surname.	Rank or Profession of Father.
1	August 1st 1914	Robert Alfred Roger	23	Bachelor	Labourer	24 Norwood Road Reading.	George Henry Roger	Baker
		Eliza Ann Matthias	21	Spinster	—	12 Castle Street Reading.	William Stephin Matthias	Tailor.

Married in the St Mary's Castle Street according to the Rites and Ceremonies of the Established Church by [Banns] after Banns by me,

This Marriage was solemnized between us, { R A Rogers / E A M atthias }   in the Presence of us, { Emily A Franklin / Walter S Matthias }   Chace Bellam

---

1914. Marriage solemnized at St Mary's Castle Street, Reading in the Parish of St Mary's in the County of Berkshire

No.	When Married.	Name and Surname.	Age.	Condition.	Rank or Profession.	Residence at the time of Marriage.	Father's Name and Surname.	Rank or Profession of Father.
2	September 12th 1914	Alfred George Hinton	35	Bachelor	Labourer	Wolhampton Hants	Chas G (deceased)	Labourer
		Jane Elizabeth Englefield	35	Spinster	—	20 Somerstown Reading	William John Englefield	Labourer

Married in the St Mary's Castle Street according to the Rites and Ceremonies of the Established Church by [Banns] after Banns by me,

This Marriage was solemnized between us, { Alfred George Hinton / Jane Elizabeth Englefield }   in the Presence of us, { Louie Holden / William John Englefield }   Jas. Chr Reading   Joan v. C

(508)

The earliest marriages solemnized in the Chapel, 1914.

WAR AND PEACE 1915-1928

It had been felt increasingly, during Mr Consterdine's time, that the absence of a parish was a hindrance to the ministry of St Mary's, Castle Street. The Chapel had enjoyed the privilege during the incumbencies of Goodhart and Tubbs of ministering to the poor folk of Coley but, with the succession of Tractarian Vicars to the Minster Church, the informal arrangements that the affable Mr Yates had been pleased to permit were not continued. Moreover, in 1875, St Mary the Virgin commenced its own work in Coley with the building of a Mission Room, followed in 1877 by an iron church and later in 1887 by the present handsome redbrick building which housed St Saviour's Church until it was closed for Anglican worship in 1985.

The possibility of a parish or conventional district being assigned to Castle Street was raised at a meeting of the Trustees in January 1914 but, perhaps on account of the outbreak of war they did not meet again until May 1915, brought together by the anticipated resignation of the incumbent. In preparation for this meeting, Thomas Hewett had canvassed the views of some of the clerical members of the Board, including Hubert Brooke, Harrington Lees and Sydenham Dixon. These were generally supportive; Brooke, for instance, drew analogies with his own situation in Brighton, where he had been nominated by the Vicar 'to the Church and conventional parish of St Margarets and the Mission District of Carlton Hill'. In submitting his resignation, Consterdine also gave his support for the principle of a conventional district. Arthur Sutton, however, in sending his apologies, drew attention to the obstacles:
'I doubt very much whether the Bishop would on his own account be willing, or on the other hand, whether he would be allowed by the High Church Party in Reading, to allot any portion of other parishes in Reading to St Mary's Episcopal, but I can quite see that without a parish it is becoming more and more difficult to get the staff of clergy which is needed.'

Thomas Hewett's account of his subsequent discussions with the Vicar of St Mary's, Rev Wickham Legg, suggested that the latter, while not unsympathetic to the Chapel's predicament, was not overjoyed at the thought of relinquishing a portion of his own parish at a time when the Town Centre population was not growing. Nevertheless, following a formal request by the Trustees, he undertook to consult with the Bishop of Oxford: 'I am sure to have a chance of seeing him soon, and I will than have a quiet word with him.' He fulfilled his promise, but then on 8 June advised the Trustees not unreasonably that it was now up to them to approach the Bishop on their own account. The ball, so to speak, was in the Trustees' court, but by this time, the imminent departure of Consterdine was much on their minds and they decided to postpone further consideration of the question till the views of his successor could be ascertained. What these were is not clear, for the matter was not raised again until 1925 — ten years and three incumbents later!

1915, marked as it was by failure to regularise the status of the Church and by the conclusion of the last incumbency to reach double figures [x], represents a watershed in the history of St Mary's, Castle Street. While four ministers had served it during its first 80 years as an Anglican church, the next 75 were to see fifteen incumbents come and go with numerous interregna intervening. As Robin Leaver puts it: 'The golden years were over and the troubled years had begun . . . From this time on there were a number of difficulties the Chapel had to face which, over the years, led to a lessening of the congregation's influence in the town and a steady decline in the numbers attending'.

The Great War also had an unsettling effect on the work of the Church. With all able-bodied men enlisting in the services, the women were left to carry on as best they could, and the destruction of so many lives in the carnage of Flanders left gaping holes in leadership in the years that followed. The War Memorial Tablet, erected in 1924, records the names of forty-one members of the Congregation and Boys' Brigade who gave their lives during 1914-18. Two prominent members of the 7th Reading, Leonard Hall and Alfred Knott, can be found among this number.

The War also had serious consequences for the spiritual life of the nation as a whole. Men were scarred mentally as well as physically and were led to question the sovereignty of God over human life and in some cases to lose their faith. Many ordinary people became less ready to accept everything they were taught as 'gospel'. In social terms, the old class society with 'the rich man in his castle, the poor man at his gate' was breaking down. The increasing grip of liberal theology on the Church of England and other mainstream denominations also contributed to the weakening of religious influence in the life of the community.

Rev Clifton David Frank Waters, formerly Curate of St Andrew's, Watford, was appointed to the incumbency on 2 September 1915 and was able to commence his ministry at the end of that month. A graduate and blue of Cambridge University, ordained in 1906, Waters came to Reading with a wife, Euphemia, and young family, to which two sons and a daughter were added during his years at Castle Street. In his letter of application for the incumbency, he stressed his belief in the substitutionary atonement, his adherence to traditional doctrines and practice in regard to the Lord's Supper, and his strong support for CMS and CPAS. He did not, however, belong to 'that school of thought which advocates the Black Gown in the pulpit and condemns all who differ'.

C.D.F. Waters was, as befitted an athlete, an energetic pastor, who was particularly effective in his youth work, in which his wife, in spite of her growing brood, also participated. He impressed young people by his earnest manner and a great many were influenced to make a commitment to Christ, including the young Bill Appleby. Bishop Gore presided at a memorable service of Confirmation on 20 March 1918 at which 79 were confirmed — 58 females and 21 males.

Wartime austerity nearly cast a blight on the Sunday School treat in 1917 when it was announced that 'in order to comply with the Food Controller's request, the children will not be provided with tea and will not therefore assemble until 4 pm'. The youngsters were, however, blessed with lovely weather and — no doubt under Mr Waters' expert guidance — 'the Sports were a great success' and 'the Cricket was appreciated even by one of the Policemen!'

Like his predecessors, Waters had a vision for 'the permanent duty of world evangelisation', so that we find him writing in the *Monthly Magazine* for August 1917:
'Just as questions of reconstruction in social and political and other affairs after the war have to be, and are being, considered now, so it is necessary that those responsible (and that should be every Christian man and woman) for Missionary enterprise, must begin to prepare now for post-war efforts.

'There is a wonderful spirit of sacrifice and service stirring now in our land, and we want to capture it, and then when the war is over, definitely turn it into Missionary directions.'

Mr Waters' incumbency was, however, but of brief duration for he left Reading at Easter 1919 to become Vicar of Mattersley, Nottinghamshire. In 1925 he became Rector of Clayworth, also in Nottinghamshire, where he spent the remainder of his ministry.

After Waters' departure, one of the most unhappy episodes in the Chapel's history commenced. This was the turbulent three-year incumbency of Frank Burnett.

The crux of the problem was that Burnett was a square peg in a round hole, a Minister who possessed or developed High Church leanings, appointed to a Church with a staunchly conservative Evangelical tradition.

The mystery is perhaps how the Trustees, who up to this point had a fine track record in selecting the right men for the job, came to make the mistake of appointing him. When they met on 30 January 1919, they had before them C. D. F. Waters' formal letter of resignation giving them three months' notice which was due to expire on Easter Day; he expressed willingness to stay on for a few days if necessary and in fact ministered for the last time on Low Sunday, 27 April. The Trustees had clearly had earlier intimation of Waters' intentions for there were already eleven applications for the vacancy. They narrowed these down to two, a former Curate of St John's, Reading and a 45-year old former Nonconformist minister, Frank Burnett, who had received Anglican orders in 1914 and was Curate of a parish in Colchester. Thomas Hewett's son, Edwin, also a Curate in Colchester at this time, was present at this meeting, but does not appear to have contributed any personal knowledge of the applicant.

Burnett, who came with strong recommendations from his Vicar and from the Bishop of Chelmsford, was favoured and invited to preach the following Sunday, 2 February, at both services. He evidently gave satisfaction: when he met the Trustees the following day he was offered and accepted the incumbency.

Frank Burnett moved into the Chapel House, with his wife, a lady with artistic talents, and their three children. The service of Institution on Sunday 4 May was conducted by Bishop Gore who preached on 'The Good Shepherd'. This must have been one of Gore's last diocesan duties, for he had already tendered his resignation to the Archbishop.

It was some time before Frank Burnetts' true colours were revealed, though an inkling that he was not a thoroughbred Evangelical could perhaps have been deduced from his tendency to base his sermons, which he liked to deliver from the high pulpit, on themes and topics rather than on Biblical texts. Some of these sound intriguing, others pretentious: 'The Anchorage', 'The High Rock', 'A Nation's Greatest Teasure', 'The Vision of the Almond Blossom', 'Imperialism', 'God's Catalogue'. At a Day of Thanksgiving for the Treaty of Versailles, his sermons were entitled 'Why we won' and 'If we had lost'. Until November 1919, we find the correct 1662 titles of the prayer book services entered into the services register, or their abbreviations, MP and EP; thereafter 'Evensong' and 'M' for Mattins appear with increasing frequency — another sign perhaps of alien sympathies.

Conflict broke out over the proposed introduction of *Hymns Ancient and Modern* in place of the *Hymnal Companion to the Book of Common Prayer*. A&M Standard Version is hardly as advanced on the path to Rome as the English Hymnal, but the incumbent's desire to switch to it was seen by some as evidence of wayward inclinations. The 'new' hymnbook was 'used for the first time by desire of the people' on 22 February 1920. Criticism of the change had already been voiced at a meeting of the Trustees on 3 February — the first anniversary of their offering Burnett the incumbency.

At this stage, however, the principal complaint before them concerned the incumbent's action in 'allowing a concert to be held in the Schoolroom (including dances)' without their prior consent. This affair seems to have been a storm in a teacup since the dances in question were the fairly innocuous Sailor's Hornpipe, performed by Mr George Dear and 'a pretty solo dance entitled "Bacca Pipes"' performed by Miss Bubbles Stark 'who won all hearts with her versatile personality'.

The hymnbook issue proved to be rather more serious, especially since Burnett had allegedly prevented the newly-formed Chapel Council from voting on the issue at a meeting specially called for that purpose the previous November. Reports were also circulating that the incumbent wished to remove the pews at the rear of the Church so that hymns from the new book could be sung in procession — an innovation clearly out of line with normal Evangelical practice.

The Trustees, therefore, felt obliged to point out to Mr Burnett the error of his ways and as a warning declined to renew their guarantee of his stipend.

Controversy continued, however, over a petition drawn up in favour of the change of hymnbook. Although the number of signatures appeared to prove that the majority of the congregation favoured A&M, no attempt had been made to restrict voting to regular attenders and members of the Chapel. That the intentions of Burnett and his hand-in-glove organist, Mr Browne, were sinister was for many confirmed when, at a service commemorating the Annunciation of the Blessed Virgin Mary, a hymn by the A&M compiler, Sir H. W. Baker, 'Shall we not love thee, Mother dear', was sung. Some of its verses clearly err in the direction of Mariolatry, though it was claimed in Burnett's defence that these had been ommitted. It was perhaps on this occasion that old Ebenezer Harding expressed his disgust by walking out of the service.

The Vestry Meeting that year saw fireworks with the resignation of both wardens, Messrs Newbery and Hewett; in the latter's case this was combined with open disapproval of the Minister's conduct. There were others, however, who stood by Mr Burnett, including the new Warden, Mr J. T. Westbrook, and the Captain of the Boys' Brigade (an organisation which Burnett to his credit had sought to build up) who argued in relation to the dancing controversy that physical culture was an important part of the nurturing of young people.

The dispute dragged on for a further two years, until the Trustees at last felt they had sufficient grounds to ask Bishop Burge of Oxford to demand the incumbent's resignation. Burnett was finally persuaded to take this course of action in June 1922. He officiated for the last time at a Communion service on St Peter's Day; the fact that there were 56 communicants present is perhaps an indication that he was by no means unloved by all his flock. The words which he inscribed across the Register of Services sum up the rather sad and sorry three years of his ministry:

'What is writ is writ — would it were worthier'.

He departed, still complaining bitterly of his treatment, especially as regards the stipend, and leaving a final legacy of his Romeward tendencies — the Communion Table was found to have been raised in height in such a way as to make it difficult for the officiating minister to adopt the north-side position required by the Prayer Book rubric. Remedial action was taken.

Burnett's new appointment, which had been arranged between the Bishops of Oxford and London as a means of defusing the situation in Reading, was the curacy of St Anne's, Stamford Hill, combined with the chaplaincy of the Prince of Wales Hospital, Tottenham. In 1925, he became Rector of Stoke St Michael, Coventry, where he remained until his retirement.

The Trustees wisely took a little more time in selecting a successor to Mr Burnett, and as a result the Church was faced with the first of the interregna referred to above. Among those who occupied the pulpit during these months was Edwin Robert Hewitt.

The man on whom the Trustees eventually settled their choice was Sydney Robert Skeens, who had been a CMS missionary in Uganda for more than twenty years. After preaching the customary test sermons on 19 November, he commenced his ministry on New Year's Day, 1923. His five years at the helm were generally less tempestuous than those of his predecessor, though his lack of sympathy for the Boys' Brigade won him a few enemies. That he was faithful in his efforts to reinvigorate the missionary interests of the church can be seen from the title of his talk to the children on his first Sunday: 'Uganda Drums'.

In 1925, Skeens revived the issue of the Chapel's status and on this occasion matters progressed as far as the appointment by Bishop Burge of a Commission to investigate the position. This comprised the Vicar of St Mary's who was now also Archdeacon of Berkshire, the Rural Dean, Skeens himself, and representatives of the Trustees, along with other prominent citizens of the town. They concluded, however, that there was no alternative at present but to continue with the status quo. The Venerable Wickham Legg, perhaps with tongue in cheek, suggested that St Mary's, Castle Street, might henceforth become known as St Matthias'. Needless to say, this idea was not accorded a rapturous welcome by the Castle Street members.

C. D. F. Waters, Minister 1915-19.

15 Ap. 1915.

Dear Mr Hewett

1. I think the main difficulty about getting a legal parish assigned to St Mary's Chapel, is the tenure of the building. That not being freehold, but under restrictions "that if-ever it were sold, the proceeds must be paid to the L.M.S." would, I think, be a complete bar.

If that restriction cd be legally removed, by the Trustees getting the deed changed & the fabric vested in the Eccl. Commissioners, only then wd the legal parish be possible.

2. But, in Brighton & elsewhere, many Churches have a Conventional district assigned to them, even if they are only Chapels of Ease, or with restrictions as to tenure of land &c. — So such an application might succeed.

3. It would then mean that the Vicar of St Mary's makes the assignment of the Conventional parish to each Incumbent of St.M.Es.Ch. on his appointment; & it is valid & officially recognized during

Extract from Hubert Brooke's Letter concerning the future of the ministry at St Mary's, Castle Street, 1915.

June 25	Trinity II	8.	H.C.	FB				15		4	8	ch. Corps	The 124th Dedication Festival
"	"	11.	Mattins & Litany	FB & HW.	Frank Burnett	Acts. 20.31		14	1	5	2	"	
"	"	6.30	Evensong	HW.	FB.	1 Kings 5.17		2	2	4	3	12	2
" 26	Monday	3.	Mothers Union	—	H. Wardley King	2 Thess: III.'							
" 29	Thursday S. Peter	8.	H.C.	Frank Burnett	—			56		-	-	no offertory	

"What is writ is writ, would it were worthier"

ABOVE: Physical culture — Boys Brigade members, including Denis Richmond and Tom Barker, setting up camp on the Isle of Wight in 1952. CENTRE: The painful end of Frank Burnett's unhappy ministry, recorded in the Chapel's Register of Services, 1922. BELOW: St Mary's Sunday School Treat in Prospect Park, 1924. Rev Sidney Skeens can be seen towards the top right.

26th day of January 1928

We the undersigned trustees of
St. Marys, Castle St. Reading.
hereby appoint the Rev: Edwin Robert Hewett
Incumbent of this Church. The appointment
to commence on the First day of March
1928:——————.

H. D. Buchanan Dunlop

W. G. Newbery

I. E. Hewitt

Jessie Flanagan

Percy R. Allen.

Allan. E. McAdam.

A C Harding.

Catherine A. Hart

Hubert Brooke

Sydenham L. Dixon

Approved, so long as the continued existence of S. Mary's
Castle Street, in its present position is inevitable.

Arthur H. Parham,
Vicar of S. Mary's, Reading.

Minute of appointment of Mr Hewett as Minister by the Trustees, 1928
INSET: Edwin Hewett, a lifelong servant of the Chapel as Trustee,
Curate and Minister.

88

Two Contrasting Ministries 1928-1946

Sydney Skeens left at the end of February 1928, having accepted the loving of Yatesbury in Wiltshire. When they met on 26 January to select his successor, the Trustees unanimously fixed their choice on Edwin Robert Hewett, moved by the recommendations of two veteran absent members, Hubert Brooke and Sydenham Dixon, and also by a letter from Catherine Hart, one of several newly-elected congregational Trustees, who was likewise unable to be present:
'We cannot speak too highly of him, for I believe his whole heart and soul are in his work and his kind and sympathetic manner has won the hearts of the people of St Mary's, Castle Street, both young and old'.

The necessary deed of appointment was drawn up, with this rather enigmatic statement added by the new Vicar of St Mary the Virgin, Arthur Groom Parham: 'Approved, so long as the continued existence of St Mary's in its present position is inevitable'.

Son and grandson of elders of the church, and himself a Trustee since 1910, Edwin Hewett had trained for the ministry at St Aidan's College, Birkenhead, during the war years, being ordained deacon in 1918 and presbyter in 1920. After serving as Curate of St Nicholas, Colchester, from 1918 to 1922 and St Paul, Erith from 1923-4, he had been honorary Curate to Mr Skeens for the past four years during which time, in Miss Hart's words, the congregation had 'been able to prove his worth'.

In spite of these promising testimonials, Edwin Hewett's ministry cannot be called a successful one. He was a person of nervous disposition, extremely shy and sensitive, and given to frequent bouts of ill-health. On the one occasion, in 1929, when he does seem to have asserted hiself, he only succeeded in dividing his flock. The trouble was caused by a dispute between Minister and Organist. Mr Browne's successor, Mr Chamberlain, had gathered together a group of artistically-minded people into a Guild of Fellowship, which met in the Schoolroom to discuss music, drama and other matters of mutual interest. Occasional disputes arose with other church organisations over such trivial issues as the use by the Guild of a piano which was claimed as the sole property of the Sunday School. As a result of one such incident, Mr Chamberlain appears to have 'lost his cool' and tendered his resignation.

Edwin Hewett took the view that the Guild of Fellowship was getting out of hand and in danger of becoming a church within a church; steps were taken to restrict its future membership to church members only. However correct this judgement may have been, one must conclude that the matter was not well handled by Mr Hewett and as a result a large number of talented people with the potential to render valuable service took Mr Chamberlain's side and dissociated themselves from the Chapel.

There were, nevertheless, positive achievements during Mr Hewett's ministry. There was one important modification to the church furnishings, which was donated by the incumbent himself. Hitherto a dark curtain had formed a rather sombre backcloth to the Communion Table. In 1929, this was replaced by the present light oak panelling bearing the inscription: 'This do in remembrance of me'. In the early '30s, there were Missions conducted by Mr Parsons from Weymouth, which were effective in building up the spiritual life of the Church.

As the thirties progressed, however, Edwin Hewett became increasingly unable to carry on his work. As early as 1931, Sydenham Dixon (a year before his death) and R. J. Hunt, on furlough from South America, were making frequent appearances in the pulpit. In 1933, the services of an honorary curate were secured. Arthur Baker, a 77-year-old retired minister and close friend of Tubbs' curate, James Hussey, shared the ministry until his death in October 1935. Another frequent visitor was Russell Berridge White (1896-1978), who had come down from Liverpool to serve as Secretary of the Evangelical Churchmen's Ordination Council. White later became Bishop of Tonbridge and was from 1968 to 1974 Chairman of the Chapel's Trustees. Oswald Goold, a later incumbent, and James Consterdine's son, Rudolph, were others who preached.

Old Thomas Hewett died in 1933 at the grand old age of 84, and his widow, Ellen, four years later. Edwin seems to have been especially affected by the loss of his beloved parents. His continued ill-health finally led him to tender his resignation to the Trustees in May 1937.

In other circumstances, the opportunity to appoint a more vigorous pastor might have been welcomed but, on the contrary, the incumbent's decision placed the Board in rather a quandary, for they had before them strong evidence that the autonomous status of St Mary's, Castle Street, was looked on with growing disfavour by certain of the hierarchy. Hewett, therefore, agreed to withdraw his resignation, on condition that a locum tenens could be secured 'for the immediate future'. As events unfolded, St Mary's had a series of locum tenentes over the next two-and-a-half years. S. V. F. Griffiths officiated during June, July and October, and Nicholas Earle during August and September. After four to five months during which Hewett himself made occasional appearances, together with guest preachers, Robert Wakefield Benson served as acting minister from March 1938 till 3 September 1939, following which there was a further helping of S. V. F. Griffiths until the arrival of a new permanent Minister.

Samuel Victor Floyd Grifiths seems to have enjoyed an almost continuous peripatetic ministry. His one regular appointment (from 1945) was the Chaplaincy of St Pancras Cemetery and he was so often seen at graveside funerals, that London cemeteries were sometimes referred to as 'Uncle Victor's gardens'. By all accounts, he was not a great preacher but he was diligent in visiting and St Mary's, Castle Street, owes much to his many spells as locum.

Mr Benson had the sorrowful duty of announcing to the congregation at his farewell service the outbreak of war with Germany. He had himself been suffering from ill-health when he arrived in Reading, but his health improved to such an extent that he was able to describe his eighteen months here as the happiest since his ordination. He went on to become Vicar of Weald in Kent.

All three locum tenentes had been willing to take on the incumbency on a permanent basis but in each case the refusal of the new Bishop of Oxford, Kenneth Kirk, to grant a full licence, prevented the appointment proceeding. Proprietary Chapels were by now regarded as an anachronism, rather as the appendix has been viewed by certain anthopologists as the vestigial survival of an earlier form of the human species. The Bishop, therefore, raised the possibility of closing down St Mary's, Castle Street and transferring its ministry to a new parish in the Southcote area which was designated by the Borough Council as an area for housing development. These possibilities had hardly been considered when the outbreak of war concentrated minds in other directions. The peculiarities of St Mary's Episcopal Chapel were forgotten and the Trustees were at last able to appoint a new Minister on terms that were acceptable to both the clergyman concerned and the Diocesan authorities. Thus it was that Sidney Saker commenced his incumbency on 3 December 1939.

After finally resigning his cure, Edwin Hewett retired from active ministry, to such an extent that he evaded the attention of most editors of *Crockford's*. For a while he resided in

Devon for the sake of his health, but continued to occupy the pulpit on occasions, especially during the interregnum of 1946-7. The Trustees, of which he remained a member till the end of his days, frequently had cause to appreciate his counsel. When he died on 30 December 1963, they 'stood in memory of the Rev E. R. Hewett, who had been called to higher service'.

At 31, Sidney Saker was one of the youngest to take up the ministry of St Mary's, Castle Street. He came to Reading four years after his ordination, having served curacies in Islington and Bermondsey. He was single at the time of his appointment, but married during his time in Reading. He took over in the middle of the Phoney War, with men of the Church once again marching off in uniform — hardly the most propitious time to commence a work for God.

Nevertheless, like C. D. F. Waters during the Kaiser's war, Mr Saker gave strong leadership at a time when it was most needed. A sound Bible man, who always carried God's Word around with him, he was especially noted for his work among youth and young adults. In this respect, he was able to build on valuable efforts by Miss Billiness in keeping together a Bible Class for young people. He would walk round the town after the evening service, drawing soldiers and other young men to attend fellowship meetings. Mr Saker was also a very practical man whose ability to mend bicycle punctures, as well as his straightforward preaching, proved attractive to young people. Mr Saker was a close friend of the noted evangelist, Tom Rees, who visited Castle Street during this period for a Keswick Mission.

From 1941, he had the assistance of a Church Army worker, Sister Stubbings, by all accounts a formidable lady. She was particularly effective in her work among the drunken and dissolute, some of whom she led to faith in Christ. On one memorable Saturday night, she knocked up the Vicar of St Mary's, Bishop Parham, and dragged him out on a pub crawl so that he could see at first hand the sort of things that went on in his parish. Some of the teacups Sister Stubbings bought for 6d at Woolworths are still in service in the Chapel's catering department.

This was also a time when St Mary's, Castle Street was blessed with Chapel Wardens from the distaff side, Miss Flanagan being succeeded in 1945 by Miss Frankum, the forthright Matron of the Battle Hospital. At least one of the post-war ministers was not entirely happy with this 'petticoat government', but Miss Frankum battled on as Warden till early in the '60s.

The Boy's Brigade enjoyed a new lease of life during the war years. With the company run down to six or seven boys, closure seemed the only option. Then, as Bill Appleby puts it: 'The matter was being discussed in the school room when there was a vigorous rat-tat at the door. Opening up, some twelve to fourteen boys stood outside. "We have come to join the Boys Brigade" they said . . . This group of boys were all evacuees from London . . . We went great guns in getting the Company going again and it was not long before . . . the echoes of bugles sounded around Castle Street calling folk to Church to hear the message of "Christ Crucified".'

Mr Saker left at the end of June 1946 to become Midlands Area Secretary of the Bible Churchmen's Missionary Society (BCMS), a new missionary concern formed in the 1920s by conservative Evangelicals who felt that CMS had become excessively liberal. He had, in Miss Frankum's words at that year's AGM, carried the Church 'through six troublesome years, which were far from free from difficulties, but in all the stress and strain' he had 'kept the flag flying, the saving of souls being always his first object'. He went on to become the South-West Area Secretary for the South American Missionary Society (SAMS) from 1953 and his last full-time appointment was with the Leprosy Mission in London from 1971-3. He now lives in retirement in Leicester.

With the post-war period we enter the most troublesome phase of the Chapel's history.

ABOVE: 7th Reading Company Boys Brigade 1940/1, including wartime evacuees. Officers in front row (L to R): William Lester, Harry Frost, Bob Evans, William Haines (Capt), Bill Appleby, Percy Frewin, Denis Richmond. LEFT: Boys Brigade on the march in Castle Street. RIGHT: Sidney Saker, Minister 1939-46.

THE CHURCH THAT WOULD NOT DIE
1946-1963

The departure of Mr Saker in 1946 heralded a long period of uncertainty for the Chapel, as a result of which the progress that had characterised his ministry was not easily sustainable. A blight was cast on the long-term future of the church building by the announcement that same year by the Borough Council of plans to build a new Civic Centre in the area bounded by Castle Street and Hosier Street, with the Chapel buildings evidently included in an area earmarked for demolition. The Council, however, was unable to give the Trustees any intimation of the timescale involved — scarcely surprising since the realisation of their plans had to wait till the 1970s.

The Trustees continued to experience Diocesan interference in the appointment of ministers. This was not entirely due to sinister intentions on the part of the hierarchy. The Bishops were faced in the aftermath of the war with a shortage of newly ordained men, with the result that they preferred to reserve younger clergymen for the regular parochial ministry.

In spite of its difficulties, Saint Mary's, Castle Street, continued to be served by a series of godly ministers, some full-time, some part-time, some permanent, others temporary. Though growth was negligible, the numbers on the electoral roll consolidated to a level of between 140 and 160 until the 1960s.

As a result of the obstructive activities of the Bishop, a fifteen-month interregnum followed the Saker era. During this period, Edwin Hewett and S. V. F. Griffiths shared the preaching ministry, with occasional appearances from Charles Richmond, Castle Street's 'Own Missionary' with BCMS, who was preparing for ordination at Bristol, and from Sidney Saker, in his new role.

In January 1947, a 28-year-old American visitor named Billy Graham, on his first evangelistic tour of Britain, made quite an impression on the young people of Reading at a rally in the Town Hall. Out of 200 who pledged commitment to Christ, twelve were from Castle Street. In the spring of that year, Arthur Harding, the much-loved People's Warden, was suddenly called home, and Dr Joseph Tinsley, a lecturer at the University, took his place. Dr Tinsley gave able and effective leadership both as Warden and Trustee during difficult and often perplexing times, until his appointment in 1958 as Head of the Department of Soil Science at Aberdeen. He remained a Trustee until 1987.

Another problem the Church faced in seeking to attract a new Minister was lack of accommodation. The previous Minister's house at 121 Castle Street had been sold to a sitting tenant and a house purchased by Edwin Hewitt's sister, Isabel, as a replacement was promptly requisitioned by the Council on account of the housing shortage. As a result of the gathering pace of inflation, the Trustees found that the funds at their disposal were insufficient to acquire a further property. Happily, Oswald Canning Goold was prepared to become a commuting parson and for his three years of ministry, commencing in September 1947, he lived at Enfield, having to make a 94-mile round trip to minister at Castle Street.

Mr Goold was an Irishman, a graduate of Trinity College, Dublin. Following his ordination in 1915, he had had experience of parochial ministry in Carlisle, Sheffield and Southport, followed by a spell as Deputation Secretary for the Sudan United Mission from 1933-40. He had been Chaplain to the RAFVR from 1942-45 and before coming to Castle Street was Vicar of St Matthew's, West Ham.

The travelling was a cause of much strain for Mr Goold and it is hardly surprising that he found difficulty in undertaking as many pastoral visits as he would have wished. He was discouraged when coming from Enfield to take a mid-week prayer meeting to find that only six people had turned up. Nevertheless, he became known as a forthright preacher, whose concern for the worldwide mission of the Church and conviction of the need to be prepared at all times for the Lord's return reminded some with long memories of Hubert Brooke; his radiant face was capable of lifting the gloomiest of hearts.

Something of the flavour of Mr Goold's preaching — the direct challenge interspersed with Celtic poetry — can be sampled in this extract from his Easter letter for 1948:
'Glad blessed Springtime of Resurrection Life, changing the barrenness of the winter of sin and death into the Spring of the Redeemed life. Thank God! The Risen Lord has changed everything for those who are redeemed by His Blood, who have found in Him the centre of life and power. Jesus died on the awful Cross of Shame that you might have cleansing from sin and eternal life . . ,
'Is it nothing to you that the Lord Jesus died and rose again to change the sin darkened life into the Sun-lit life in the Risen Lord? . . . The Resurrection of our Lord is the greatest, grandest fact in history and it should be so in your life. Have you a song to sing this glorious Eastertide?'

1948 was also the year in which the Chapel's 150th Anniversary was celebrated. The guest preachers at special services, held in the summer, rather than near the Anniversary date of 16 December, were Charles Richmond and Rudolph Consterdine. An appeal for £650 for improvements to the heating system was made in connection with the Anniversary.

Mr Goold left in May 1950 to resume missionary deputation work. After three years in the service of Irish Church Missions, he returned to the Sudan United Mission in 1953.

Problems were again encountered in the appointment of a replacement and another lengthy interregnum ensued. Once more, the faithful S. V. F. Griffiths was in evidence, but the brunt of the ministry during this period was borne by Rev Frederick Augustus Watney, a retired clergyman, ordained as early as 1902, who lived at Burghfield Common. Yet another mission-minded man, he had worked for what is now CMJ from 1909-15 and was one of the founder-members of BCMS. During a second period of acting incumbency in 1953, at the ripe age of 74, he married a member of the congregation, Miss M. Crosse of Castle Hill. He served as a Trustee from 1956-69, and such was his affection for St Mary's, Castle Street, that he later gave elaborate instructions for his funeral service to be held in the Chapel.

In February 1951, the Trustees were at last able to get round the Diocese's objections to releasing young Church of *England* ministers by appointing a young *Englishman* who had been ordained into the Church of *Ireland!* This was Michael Willoughby Dewar, who was not able to commence his brief ministry until five months later. He described himself as 'a convinced evangelical Protestant, believing that the Holy Scriptures and the Thirty Nine Articles are the foundation deeds of the Church of England (and Ireland) and that the Gospel is still "the power of salvation to everyone that believeth".' He also claimed to be a 'Hampshire Hog', to whom Reading was 'no strange land'.

Michael Dewar had been educated in Devon, at Blundells School, Tiverton, where he won prizes for history, continuing his studies at Emmanuel College, Cambridge. These were interrupted by war service in the Intelligence Corps. One of his more unusual wartime jobs was that of interpreter between the Allied Chaplains and the French Reformed Church. After graduating in 1947 in Anglo-Saxon and Old Norse, he studied for the ministry at Birkenhead and was then ordained in 1949 to the middle curacy of Shankill Parish Church, Lurgan, County Armagh.

Though happy in his work among the mill-owners and linen-workers of Lurgan, he had been looking for a move to the mainland so that he could more easily study for a PhD in 16th/17th century church history. His letter applying for the incumbency of Castle Street crossed with one from the Trustees, inviting him to consider the appointment! By the time Mr Dewar arrived, the housing problems had been ironed out, with No 17 Mansfield Road ready to become the latest of the many parsonages inhabited by incumbents of the Chapel. Michael Dewar's patriotic sense of the importance of history and in particular the continuing relevance of the Reformation, can be seen in the Accession sermon which he reprinted in the *Church Magazine* for March 1952:

'The British Monarch is as surely ordained to his or her calling as any clergyman. Dedicated to the service of God and Country, our Sovereigns declare at the very threshold of their reigns, "I am a faithful Protestant". Receiving the Holy Bible, as "the most precious thing this world affords", another Sword, "the Sword of the Spirit, which is the Word of God", is carried together with the Swords of State to Westminster. This custom, enshrining the Bible at the very heart of our national life, was introduced by the young Edward VI, "the English Josiah", in whose reign the Holy Reformation first took root in England'.

Mr Dewar's time in Reading was, however, destined to be brief. He found difficulty in supporting a wife and young son on an income intended to reward a part-time ministry and accepted a curacy in Belfast. His short but memorable incumbency of St Mary's, Castle Street was concluded on 31 August 1952, when he preached on the text from the 121st Psalm, 'I will lift my eyes up unto the hills, from whence cometh my help'.

The remainder of Mr Dewar's parochial ministry was largely spent in Ulster, latterly (1973-86) as incumbent of Helen's Bay in the Diocese of Down and Dromore. Since his retirement, Canon Dr Dewar has lived in Cheltenham and a number of members of the present congregation had the pleasure of hearing his address at a service held in London to mark the 300th Anniversary of the Glorious Revolution of 1688. His considerable learning has also been in evidence at lighter moments, as when he became 'Brain of Britain'.

The interregnum following Michael Dewar's return across the Irish Sea was of 13 months' duration, but at least the congregation was able to settle down under two substantial acting incumbencies: Mr Watney returned for eight months until May 1953 and a friend of his, Rev Edmund Dunn, then looked after the ministry until the arrival of a new incumbent in October.

After a number of false starts, the Trustees were at last able to appoint Rev Frederick Harold Peacock, whose incumbency just short of eight years has been the longest since that of Edwin Hewett.

Harold Peacock was 48 at the time of his arrival in Reading. In his younger days he had pursued a career in business and was then a member of the editorial staff of the *Christian Herald* for several years before his call to the ministry. This was almost an inevitable event since he came of a churchy family, with father, grandfather, great-grandfather all clergymen, and a brother and an uncle too; as if that was not enough, his wife's father and three uncles were also in holy orders. Mr Peacock senior had been incumbent of one of the other surviving proprietary chapels, Holy Trinity, Buxton.

After studying at the London College of Divinity, Harold Peacock was ordained in 1940 and, after a curacy in Parkstone, Dorset, served for ten years as Vicar of Hennock, near Newton Abbot in Devon.

In Reading, he became known for his open and direct preaching of the Gospel and for sound Biblical exposition. An intriguing series of sermons delivered in 1957 concerned the Bonfires of the Bible (with the notable exclusion of the Burning Bush!; April 1961 was marked by a highly topical sermon entitled 'The First Spaceman's Testimony' with a text from Genesis 1. The period of stable ministry under Mr Peacock helped to consolidate St Mary's, Castle Street, at a time when things might otherwise have disintegrated completely; when he left the electoral roll still stood at 143 in spite of the passing of many of the older members of the congregation.

Continuing funding difficulties, compounded by the delapidated state of the church fabric, led to serious consideration in 1955/6 to closing the Chapel and moving to a new parish site. Some of the Trustees were moved by the thought that had they been able to proceed with the Bishop's proposal in 1939 concerning a move to Southcote, there might by now be a flourishing Evangelical witness there; as it was, not one of parishes established in the new housing estates to the west and south-west of Reading town centre was served by an Evangelical ministry.

There was, however, a strong conflict of opinion among the Trustees. Although there were signs that any proposals the Board put forward would receive sympathetic consideration by the Diocesan authorities, some members were fearful that, in spite of the cast-iron provisions of the Trust Deed, the new Church of England canons then under preparation could undermine the conservative Evangelical tradition guaranteed in the Deed. Edwin Hewett, in particular, argued that the 'advantages of independence outweighed those to be gained by becoming a parish church', and even cited his personal conviction of the imminence of the Lord's return as a reason for staying put! Harold Peacock himself was not an enthusiast for the proposed move and was able to point to encouraging signs of progress in the Castle Street ministry. As a result consideration of change in the status of the Chapel was once again deferred.

The immediate financial difficulties were resolved by the sale of the old episcopal school and a property in St Mary's Butts. The transactions involving the former raised over £3,000 and required complex negotiations with the Charity Commissioners. The sums raised enabled essential works to be carried out including the complete re-roofing of the Church, the provision of a new kitchen and toilets and the replacement of the old (and rather explosive) coal-fired boiler with an oil-fired model. The condition of the Bell Tower also gave rise to concern and eventually, towards the end of 1959, it was dismantled. Earlier, in 1957, the Church had been listed by the Ministry of Housing and Local Government as a building of historic and architectural interest and the likelihood that it would bow before the bulldozer was thus diminished.

Mr Peacock suffered much ill-health during 1959-60. The latest Minister's house at 56 Tilehurst Road, which was not noted for its mod. cons., probably did not facilitate a speedy recovery. At last, in 1961, he felt obliged to retire from the incumbency, preaching for the last time on 28 May. He did not take on further pastoral work after leaving Reading, but was, nevertheless, blessed with a long life, being called home in June 1988.

St Mary's, Castle Street, did not have quite as long as usual to wait for a new Minister after Mr Peacock's departure. Rev Dr Frederick Thomas Ellis commenced his Ministry just before Christmas 1961. During the intervening months the pulpit was occupied by such old friends as Griffiths, Watney, Saker and R. Consterdine. The service of welcome to Dr Ellis on 15 December 1961 was conducted by Castle Street's 'own Bishop', Rt Rev Russell White.

Dr Ellis, who had been ordained relatively late in life, in 1945, had served his curacy at Christ Church, Beckenham, and had then been Vicar of St Peter's, Tunbridge Wells from 1948-51 and thereafter of St Cuthbert's, West Hampstead. Christ Church had been Harrington Lees' parish from 1907 to 1919, while St Peter's was until their recent retirement home of John and Barbara Hurst. Dr Ellis was well-known as a Convention speaker on both sides of the Atlantic and as author of a number of booklets on Biblical subjects; he came to Reading with a view to developing evangelistic outreach in the town centre.

He was, however, a sick man, with chronic bronchitis and, as in the last years of Mr Peacock, his two years' Ministry was much interrupted by ill-health, particularly during the winter months. He was probably ill-advised to come to the Thames Valley, but such was his dedication to God's cause that considerations of that nature were laid aside. His ministry among teenagers was especially well-blessed and some of the young people he touched even sought to start their own prayer-meeting.

The Chapel as well as the Minister suffered from the severe cold spell of early 1963 and for several months services had to be adjourned to the Schoolroom. Dr Ellis felt that he could not face another winter in Reading and gave notice of his intention to retire to Norwich where some of his family were living. He did not long survive his departure from Reading, which took effect from 10 November 1963.

Harold Peacock, longest-serving post-war Minister 1953-61.

Interior of St Mary's, Castle Street, prior to reordering in 1972.

THE WOODLEY INTERLUDE 1964-1970

The interregnum after Dr Ellis' departure was of short duration, for the Trustees, who were starting to reconsider the Chapel's future, decided to appoint a part-time incumbent for a six-month experimental period. This was Rev Bryan Edwin Hardman, an Australian, who had recently taken on the Editorship of the Anglican newspaper, the *English Churchman*.

After studying at Moore Theological College, Sydney, Mr Hardman had been ordained in 1955 and, after a curacy in his native land, had come to England in 1957 to pursue his studies at the London Bible College. He commenced his ministry in Reading on 8 March 1964.

The Trustees were once again faced with domestic problems, as it was now clear that the Tilehurst Road property was unsuitable as a parsonage. They acquired a house in Burghfield Road with the assistance of a legacy left by Edwin Hewett and the proceeds of the sale of 56 Tilehurst Road forwarded by Miss Hewett.

Mr Hardman was sufficiently encouraged by the first few months to tell the Trustees he would be prepared to take on a full-time appointment; his contract on a part-time basis was renewed from 1 October. Shortly afterwards, however, financial problems at the *English Churchman* developed which compelled him to resign from the incumbency. Although his resignation had been timed to take effect from Easter 1965, Mr Hardman remained in post until well into July.

He was noted for the rather hard line he took on certain issues such as the placing of flowers on the Lord's Table and the restriction of infant baptism to the children of regular worshippers. It was also during his time that the Chapel became a member of the Evangelical Alliance.

After leaving Reading, Bryan Hardman served as Vicar of St Andrew the Less, Cambridge, during which time he obtained a PhD. He then returned to Australia in 1968, to become Vice-Principal of the Adelaide Bible Institute.

After the Trustees had looked at a number of other possibilities, the vacant incumbency was finally offered to Rev Gordon Murray, who had been appointed to succeed Bryan Hardman at the *English Churchman*. In spite of their earlier difficulties, the proprietors were able to offer Mr Murray a three-year contract on satisfactory financial terms; the Chapel was thus assured of the continuity of ministry that had been lacking since the retirement of Mr Peacock. Mr Murray was aged 32 and married with a young family. Converted during National Service, he had served curacies at Hereford and Weston-super-Mare before coming to Reading. Eric Knell, who had succeeded Arthur Groom Parham as Bishop of Reading in 1955, was present at a service of introduction on 24 October 1965.

Mr Murray resided at yet another new parsonage, located in a part of Earley close to the University campus with the rather profane street-name of Falstaff Avenue. From there he used to cycle down to Castle Street, three times of a Sunday, often carrying two of his children on the crossbar.

He was especially effective in his work with children and young people; a Pathfinders class for teenagers was begun during his time.

Towards the end of 1967, however, Gordon Murray accepted the appointment of Principal of Kensit Bible College, London, and his ministry in Reading came to an end the following Easter. Subsequently, he became disillusioned by the doctrinal drift in the Church of England and entered the Baptist ministry. The erosion of the reformed doctrines of the Church of England had been a matter of concern to the Chapel Council during his time at Castle Street when the experimental Series II services authorised such unscriptural practices as prayers for the dead in public worship. Gordon Murray is now Minister of a Baptist congregation at Felixstowe in Suffolk; several members of Saint Mary's, Castle Street had the opportunity of renewing fellowship with him when he returned to Reading in 1984 to take part in a Good Friday Bible Rally held at Carey Baptist Church.

Since the appointment of a successor to Mr Murray was intimately bound up with the plans the Trustees had been developing for the Chapel's future, it is now necessary to turn back the pages of history a few years to trace their progress.

The question had first resurfaced during Dr Ellis' Ministry. At that time, the Trustees included two Bishops in their ranks, Russell White of Tonbridge and Gordon Savage (1915-90) of Buckingham, who later became Diocesan Bishop of Southwell. These two, it was felt, would be helpful in cutting through the hierarchical red tape. Furthermore, Eric Knell of Reading and Harry Carpenter of Oxford both enjoyed the reputation of being fair-minded bishops, who were not disposed to show less favour to Evangelicals than to Anglo-Catholics.

Following an encouraging report by Bishop Savage which concluded that any approach made by the Trustees would receive a sympathetic hearing, it was agreed in principle, at a meeting on 18 March 1963, to explore the possibility of removing the Church to a new area of mission, possibly on the basis of joint-patronage with the Church Pastoral Aid Society (CPAS).

Even having come this far, the Trustees still moved cautiously, knowing that there were as yet a number of imponderables: the future plans of the Borough Council were still uncertain, an equivocal reply having been received to the latest enquiry; and the Charity Commissioners' interpretation of the implications of the Trust Deed for the proposed move had to be ascertained. Last but not least, there was the need to carry the worshipping congregation with them. While it was known that some of the older and less mobile members would not wish to move with the Church and would be sorry to see 'the old place' closed down, it was felt that some of the younger, who already tended to live at a distance from Castle Street, might be filled with enthusiasm for the new project.

The need to find a successor, first for Dr Ellis, then for Bryan Hardman, also slowed progress, but preliminary discussions with the Bishop showed that he was 'very interested' and enquiries to the Charity Commissioners revealed no obstacles from those quarters. Finally, at a meeting between the Trustees and the Chapel Council on 26 March 1965, the latter gave their support.

At first, Caversham Park appeared to be the most likely site for a 'new' St. Mary's, but rumours of plans for a multi-denominational church centre there were discouraging. Eventually, in January 1967, the Bishop informed the Trustees that housing develoments in that area had ceased for the time being and Woodley now looked a more promising venue.

Woodley was then being developed as a separate town with a population of 29,000, but in 1967 it was served by one Anglican church, St John's, built in 1873, as well as the tiny Congregational Chapel established by James Sherman. The Vicar of St John's, Rev H. W. H. Wilkinson, felt quite unable to cater for the needs of the new area of development around the South Lake and, although himself of a different churchmanship, was happy for a team of workers from Castle Street to start visiting on the new estate in order to 'test the waters'. Though he saw this work as leading to a conventional district rather than a separate parish, and the extent to which any eventual church development in bricks and mortar would be funded by the Diocese remained a mystery, the people of St Mary's, Castle Street, decided to go forth in faith, as had their predecessors under James Sherman 140 years ealier.

Richard Sutton, a member of the seeds family, who was also a Lay Reader at Castle Street, took the lead in visiting the area, to such good effect that by January 1968 it was possible to start up a Pathfinder Class and anticipate a Sunday School for 100 children.

Encouraged by the progress in Woodley, the Trustees decided to appoint a full-time Minister with responsibility for running down the work at Castle Street — if this was seen to be God's will — and building up the work in Woodley. With this end in view, the parsonage in Earley was sold and one in Campbell Road in the South Lake area of Woodley was acquired to house the new incumbent.

The man chosen was Dennis Parker, Curate of Polegate in Sussex, a 45-year-old who had been ordained as recently as 1964, having previously pursued a teaching career. With the assistance of a grant from CPAS and pledges given by members of the congregation, the Trustees were able to offer a stipend that was adequate to the dual responsibilities.

The work in Woodley continued to flourish and a young schoolteacher, David Karsten, joined in the lay ministry there and took over the leadership when Richard Sutton left to train for ordination. At the same time, however, the work in Castle Street showed signs of revival rather than runing down, with a number of able, professional people being attracted into membership and several of the older members remaining firmly committed to the Chapel's survival. Dennis Parker found himself in the rather invidious position of having to devote most of his energies to Castle Street, while living in Woodley, where he was hampered by having no recognised pastoral authority.

The growing will to continue the Town Centre Ministry in Reading, coupled with uncertainty how — even if the old building could be sold — any enterprise in Woodley was to be financed, led the Trustees to withdraw from the project in October 1969. While this was disappointing to some of those closely involved, it was clear that, while the church authorities were content for St Mary's, Castle Street, to beaver away in Woodley, they were less prepared to guarantee financial support; the Trustees really had little choice but to call it a day.

So, was a great opportunity missed? By no means. Castle Street had given a great boost to green-field evangelistic work in Woodley, and several of those who had been involved, including David Karsten, continued to devote their energies to building on those foundations. In February 1972, they were at last able to announce that they were completing the purchase of the site for a church, the likely name of which was St James'. St James' has remained a daughter church of St John's, but these two sons of thunder are now both served by an Evanglical ministry. Castle Street retains its links through David Karsten's continuing service as a Trustee of the Chapel.

Moreover, the part the Chapel had played in spearheading the work in Woodley had enhanced its standing in the eyes of the Diocese, which was now less inclined to regard it as belonging to a species nearing extinction. The future of St Mary's, Castle Street, in spite of several crises yet to come, did at last seem assured and its people, though by now a small remnant, became confident that under God it still had a role to play in an important area of the town.

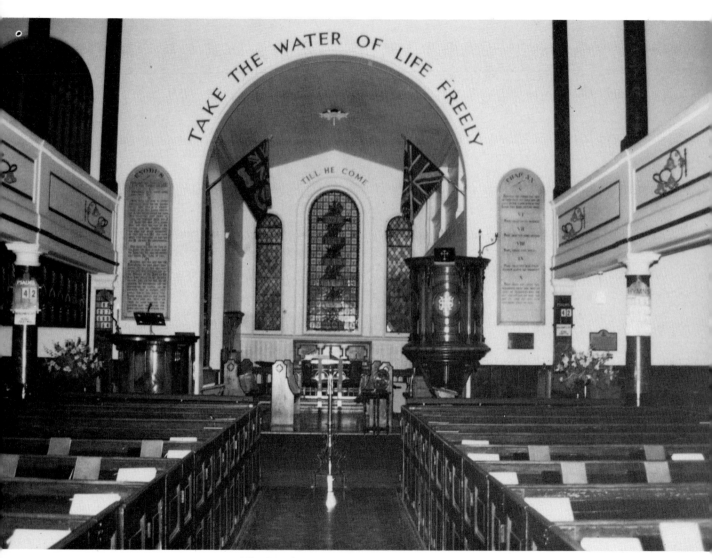

The Interior of the Chapel as it appears at present. (ES)

A NEW LEASE OF LIFE

1970 to the present

Not long after the decision to withdraw from direct involvement in Woodley, Dennis Parker accepted the living of Newdigate in Surrey. His two years' ministry at Castle Street concluded on 21 June 1970; that at Newdigate saw him through to retirement in 1987.

In the space of a decade, St Mary's, Castle Street, had thus achieved the unenviable distinction of saying goodbye to five incumbents. The next twenty years, however, comprised three substantial incumbencies, together with two rather lengthy fifties-style interregna.

The first of these followed Mr Parker's move to Surrey. There was no regular pulpit supply during this period, but neither was it a time of standing still. In the faith that the Chapel would live on, the complete redecoration of the interior was undertaken, so that it took on much the appearance that it has today. A Service of Thanksgiving was held on Friday 13 November, with the late John Swinbank, a Trustee, then Chaplain of Bradfield College, as preacher. On 28 January following, a more solemn gathering occurred with the funeral of Isabel Mary Hewett. Such had been the contribution of her family to the life of the Church over nearly 150 years that the passing of the 'last of the Hewetts' must have seemed like the end of an era. She had been a generous benefactress of the Chapel during her life and bequeathed it a further £1,500 in her will.

A rise in the Diocesan stipend, together with their perennial financial pressures, caused the Trustees to think once again in terms of a part-time minister. Eventually, their choice was fixed on the 32-year-old Robin Leaver, who wanted to combine part-time ministry with the pursuit of his scholarly interest in the theology and music of the Reformation. Mr Leaver completed major works on Marbeck and Bach during his time at Castle Street. He also found the time to research the history of his new cure. The present writer is greatly indebted to his *Short History of Saint Mary's Chapel, Castle Street, Reading* (1973) and also to the material he gathered together with a view to compiling a longer account, which did not come to fruition.

Saint Mary's had become rather run down numerically when Mr Leaver began his incumbency in October 1971. With all the uncertainty, Easter communicants had fallen to 20 in 1970. When the Borough Council finally pronounced on the last day of March 1972 that, far from forming part of their redevelopment scheme, the Chapel was regarded as a building of primary importance in a conservation area, the revival of the Town Centre Ministry of St Mary's, Castle Street, could get under way.

Robin Leaver encouraged the idea of the Church as a family, revived the Sunday School, introduced sermon series and worship themes, and began the 10 am Sunday morning prayer meeting initially called 'Open to God'. These innovations encouraged a number of younger families into church membership.

Modifications to the interior were carried out in 1972 with the construction of a dais forward of the chancel arch as the main area for the conduct of services including Communion. A new set of Communion rails, given in memory of Arthur and Jessie Harding, was placed across the dais and the choir stalls moved back into the chancel. The old organ, which was in a lamentable state, was taken out of commission (though it remained on site till 1986) and an Allen Computer Organ was acquired, partly paid for out of Isobel Hewett's bequest.

In 1973, the Chapel celebrated its 175th birthday. Robin Leaver's musicology undoubtedly helped in the planning of the celebrations, which included performances of the two oratorios referred to in previous chapters. The preachers at special services included the new Bishop of Reading, Eric Wild, Bishop Russell White, and Dr James Packer of Trinity College, Bristol, along with former ministers Saker, Murray and Parker, and clergy from neighbouring Evangelical churches.

A year later, such was the state of the fabric that the Trustees felt obliged to issue a public appeal for £7,150 for restoration of the stonework, woodworm treatment and roof repairs. The appeal leaflet included a message from the Poet Laureate who declared:

'I am pleased to support this Appeal for two reasons. The portico of St Mary's is a welcome and vital feature to the townscape of Reading's mercifully spared Castle Street. The church itself is a curious and rare survival and appeals to

Yours sincerely

John Betjeman

2 December 1974.'

Generous contributions totalling £4,000 were made by the Historic Churches Preservation Trust, the Civic Trust and the Historic Buildings Council, though it was not until 1977 that work could be put in hand. Further thought was also given to the adaptation of the buildings to the present needs of the congregation and various schemes were promulgated for demolishing the chancel and schoolroom and replacing them with a modern block comprising part-church and part-living/office accommodation and for closing off the area under the rear gallery to provide meeting rooms. None of these came to fruition, though it is scarcely deniable that the Victorian additions to the Chapel are past their prime.

Mr Leaver left in January 1977, to take up an appointment with Latimer House, Oxford, combined with the incumbency of St Mary the Virgin, Cogges, near Witney. He continued to develop his musical/theological scholarship and is currently engaged in academic work in this field in the USA.

In spite of the good impression left over from the Woodley episode, Mr Leaver's departure ushered in another period of uncertainty in the Chapel's relationship with the Diocese. Bishop Wild was known to be a man of pronounced Anglo-Catholic views, who might not be sympathetic to its Evangelical tradition. He was not as inimical as might have been feared, but at a time when pastoral reorganisation was coming into vogue he did want to see Castle Street integrated into the Anglican ministry in Reading. At first, he had thoughts of reviving an earlier proposal, that had gone down like the proverbial lead balloon, of making the Chapel a daughter church of Greyfriars. Some Trustees were in favour of this suggestion, but the majority considered that such a step would lead to total absorption and loss of identity. Early in 1977, the Bishop proposed that the incumbency should be combined with the post of Social Responsibility Officer for the Reading Deanery. Howver, the job description of this post was somewhat vague and failed to attract any of the candidates interested in the incumbency.

The Bishop's interventions only had the effect of delaying the choice of a new Minister. Eventually, the Trustees appointed a retired priest of pensionable age on a part-time basis for three years, with a view to making a full-time permanent appointment, once plans to capitalise on the market potential of the Chapel House had been implemented.

During the interregnum, the congregation was fortunate in having the regular ministry of Rev John Hanbury Hill, who had helped occasionally during Mr Leaver's time and continued to assist with the pulpit ministry until his passing early in 1980.

The part-time Minister chosen was Rev Cyril Theodore Martin Browne, whose saintly and episcopal names must have marked him out for the Ministry. Mr Browne had been born in Canada in 1912, but came to England in the 1920s and trained for the ministry at Bristol. After ordination in 1935, he served for most of the next forty years in London with the exception of a brief curacy in Worthing. He was Perpetual Curate of Muswell Hill from 1943-50 and subsequently Vicar of parishes in Clerkenwell and Greenwich. Prior to the commencement of his ministry in Reading on 28 May 1978, he had held two rural livings near Malpas, Cheshire.

A bachelor, he brought with him to Reading his sister, Eunice, and their housekeeper and companion, Miss Iris Dodd, who both became closely involved in the activities of the Chapel. Iris in particular was able to assist in the pastoral work, such as the Women's Fellowship. She also served as an officer in the 1st Caversham Girls' Brigade and was a courier for the Bible-smuggling organisation, Open Doors. She and Miss Browne, however, both died towards the end of Mr Browne's ministry.

Mr Browne himself will be remembered for his kindly, gentle manner which endeared him to young and old alike. The revival, commenced under Robin Leaver, continued steadily, if unspectacularly, during his incumbency. Like some of his predecessors with a similar designation, he was far more than a part-time Minister and when he left he had served for longer than any of the post-war ministers apart from Mr Peacock.

Early in 1983, the Trustees announced that they could now see their way clear to the appointment of a younger man on a full-time and fully-salaried basis. However, the selection process was, as so often, beset by problems and lasted for over a year. Mr Browne willingly soldiered on and when his ministry finally came to an end on 6 May 1984 he had served just a few weeks short of six years. Many of his friends would have liked him to stay in Reading, but he felt compelled to seek other spheres of service. After five years in charge of a village church at Stockton near Southam in Warwickshire, he moved to Tunbridge Wells, where he is still active in providing assistance to local clergy.

His successor, Allan Harold Leslie Bowhill, was licensed to the cure of souls at St Mary's, Castle Street, by the new Bishop of Reading, Graham Foley, on 14 May 1984.

A 41-year-old ex-policeman, Mr Bowhill had only been in the ordained ministry for two years prior to his arriving at Castle Street, during which time he had served as Curate to his brother-in-law, Rev Edward Malcolm, at St Luke's, Wolverhampton. A link was found to exist between the churches, through Mr Malcolm's father, George, who had been Curate of Greyfriars through the war years and preached in the Chapel a number of times during Mr Saker's incumbency; both father and son had served as BCMS missionaries.

A further connection with St Mary's, Castle Street, was through Rev S. V. F. Griffiths, whose brother, Selwyn, was Vicar of St Mark's, Tollington Park, in North London, where Allan Bowhill first heard the Gospel as a boy.

Allan Bowhill himself had lived an adventurous life prior to his ordination, with spells in the Army and the CID, including a period as a military policeman and service in Aden during the troubles. After four years working for the Forestry Commission in the West Country at a time when he was beginning to experience the call to the Ministry, he had gone out to Port Moresby in Papua New Guinea in 1977 to establish the Ports Police there.

On his return he underwent training for ordination at Trinity College, Bristol. Several of Mr Bowhill's sermons were flavoured by his experiences as soldier and detective.

He brought with him to Reading his wife, Beverley, and a son and two daughters, all of young adult age; the whole family became active members of the Church, though both daughters later married and moved away.

The six years of Mr Bowhill's ministry saw a growth in the size of the congregation, with the electoral roll passing 70. The outreach of the Church to the community developed, with an active pre-school play group the most noticeable outwardly visible sign.

In 1985, the first Confirmation held in the Chapel for many years took place, with Bishop Foley returning to conduct the rite. The following year, the Chapel celebrated the 150th anniversary of its reception into the Establishment; appropriately the preacher on this occasion was Rev Maurice Handford, then Minister of Holy Trinity, Buxton.

In 1987, the Church was able to acquire, through the good offices of Dr Christopher Kent of Reading University, the pipe organ from the redundant Clifton United Reformed Church in Bristol. This instrument, a Vowles, dating from 1870, proved almost a perfect fit for the old organ chamber, when reinstalled by the organ-builder, Roger Taylor. A choir had already reformed under the leadership of Andrew Mannings, who was succeeded as Choirmaster in 1988 by Gordon Spriggs, formerly of Greyfriars.

The Chapel gave financial support to Andrew Mannings and his family when they moved up to Stalybridge in Cheshire early in 1988. Andrew's mission was to help build up the run-down parish of St James, Millbrook. This proved to be a most successful venture and led to Andrew's acceptance for training for the ministry. In 1992, he was ordained to the diaconate and commenced his duties in the parish of St Luke's, Over, in the Chester Diocese.

In 1988, the Church was also able to offer a lay pastorate to Mark Jones, who had recently returned with his wife, Isobel, from two years' short-term service with BCMS in Kenya, where they worked as teachers. The church benefited greatly from Mark's nine months of ministry, the early part of which coincided with a serious illness suffered by Allan Bowhill from which by God's grace he recovered. Another whose preaching gifts were encouraged by Mr Bowhill was Peter Simpson who has since become Minister of Penn Free Methodist Church.

The eighties saw the loss of several well-loved older members of the Chapel including Bill Appleby, Ted Kibble, Harry Frost and Mrs Smith, and the untimely death following a car accident of Mr David Welch, a great spiritual force in the Church, who had been Chapel Warden from 1975-83. David's widow, Jane, has produced a beautiful set of Communion kneelers featuring plants and animals of the Bible.

Early in the new decade, Allan Bowhill announced his imminent departure to Somerset and on 7 September he was inducted by the Bishop of Taunton into the livings of Keinton Mandeville and Lydford-on-Fosse; a substantial contingent from Castle Street was among those who squeezed into the modestly-proportioned village church at Lydford.

Shortly afterwards, the Trustees were able to announce the choice of Rev Dr David Samuel, as successor to Mr Bowhill. Dr Samuel was licensed to the incumbency at a service on 21 February 1991, at which the present Bishop of Reading, John Bone, presided.

David Samuel was born in Swansea in 1930, the son and grandson of Baptist ministers and himself entered the Baptist Ministry before taking Anglican Orders in 1961. He had been Director of the Church Society for seven years before coming to Reading and prior to that had spent fifteen years in rural ministry in Lincolnshire. During this period he was also Secretary of the Protestant Reformation Society. He is a distinguished scholar whose writing includes *Pope or Gospel*, as well as pamphlets on Reformed issues. Some of these interests have been reflected in the institution of an annual One-Day Conference, the first of which was held in the Chapel in October 1991.

I began this account with the intention of emphasising the role of the laity, which is sometimes neglected in church histories written by clerics. I am conscious, however, that in naming some of those who are still among the Lord's saints in Castle Street and not others, I have laid myself open to the charge of making invidious comparisons. Even so, this story would certainly not be complete without a mention of Mrs Ethel O'Neill, a sprightly 86-year-old, who was baptized and married at Castle Street, and who has served on the Chapel Council for much of her adult life. She gave many years of service, too, in the Sunday School and has been a faithful supporter of Bible study and prayer meetings week by week. St Mary's, Castle Street, owes much to people like Mrs O'Neill who have stuck with it through thick and thin; they have been the instruments by which the Lord God has preseved this place that it may be of service to a later generation.

The Church that had its origins in the faithful preaching of Talbot and Cadogan has indeed refused to die, partly because, as it must have appeared to the ecclesiastical authorities, of the stubborn independence of its members, but far more because of their conviction that it had been built for a purpose that still remained. 'Proclaiming the Gospel since 1798' is the proud claim restated on the Chapel's Notice Board. This is indeed our purpose: 'We preach Christ Crucified'. As Bishop J. C. Ryle's words chosen to form part of the title page of this book remind us, this is the message that keeps a church alive. The Church that is faithful to that calling to proclaim the Gospel is indeed part of that universal church, built on the rock of Jesus Christ, which shall·remain 'Till He Come'.

15 January 1990 - 24 January 1993

THE WELL HOUSE,
UPPER BASILDON,
READING,
BERKSHIRE
RG8 8TU

4th April, 1978

Dear Mr. Appleby,

    Thank you for your letter of 31st March about the procedure for Licensing Mr. Browne on 28th May. I take it that the service will be at 6.30 p.m.

    I note that you suggest that we use Evensong as the preliminary to the Licensing, but I should prefer this to be done within the setting of the Holy Communion. There is a special form of service in use at Institutions, but this is not applicable in your case. In similar situations I always Licence the priest in the setting of the Holy Communion, and I should be most grateful to have your observations on this matter so far as St. Mary's, Castle Street, is concerned.

    I am telling the Rural Dean about this event as I know that he will wish to be present if he possibly can.

    All good wishes,

        Yours sincerely,

        Eric Reading.

E. Appleby Esq.,
5 Norris Road,
Reading RG6 1NJ.

Letter from Bishop Eric Wild concerning arrangements for Mr Browne's licensing Service, 1978.

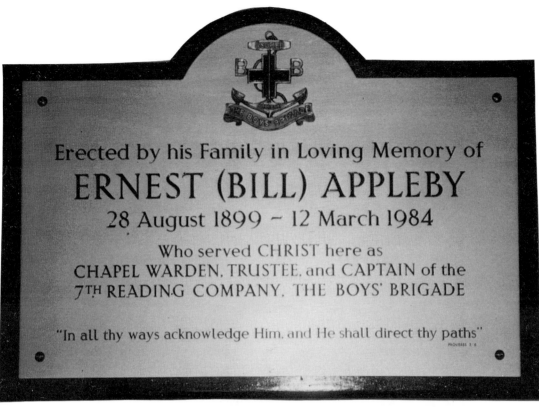

ABOVE: Memorial Tablet to Bill Appleby in St Mary's, Castle Street.
(ES) BELOW: An almost perfect fit: the 'new' organ installed in 1987.
(ES)

BIBLIOGRAPHY

The following are the principal books that have been consulted by the author in compiling this history:

Allon, H. *Memoir of the Rev. James Sherman,* 1864

Arnold, H. G. *Victorian Architecture in Reading,* 1976
   (with Gold, S. M.), *Morris of Reading,* 1989

Ayres, May and Sanders, K. J. *As Stupid as Oxen,* 1989

Balleine, G. R. *A History of the Evangelical Party in the Church of England,* 1908

Brooke, H. *The Fact and Features of the Lord's Return,* 1911

Carus, W. *Memoirs of the Life of the Rev. Charles Simeon, M.A.* 1847

Cecil, R. *Memoirs of W. B. Cadogan,* 1798

Cole, Sonia. *Leakey's Luck,* 1975

Colvin, H. *Biographical Dictionary of British Architects 1600-1840,* 1978

Consterdine, J. *Early History of St Mary's Castle Street, Reading,* 1903

Cooke, J. *Five Letters to a Friend,* 1797

Cusden, Phoebe. *Coley, portrait of an urban village,* 1977

Darter, W. *Reminiscences of Reading,* 1889

Doran, J. *History and Antiquities of the Town and Borough of Reading in Berks,* 1835

Gauntlett, Catherine *Memoir of Revd. H. Gauntlett,* 1835

Gauntlett, H. *Letters to the Stranger in Reading by Detector,* 1810

Gidney, W. T. *History of the London Society for Promoting Christianity among the Jews,* 1908

Harman, L. *The Parish of St Giles in Reading,* 1946

Hole, C. *Life of the Rev. and Ven. William Whitmarsh Phelps, MA,* 1871

Jones, J. B. *Sketches of Reading,* 1870

Knight, Helen *Lady Huntingdon and Friends,* 1853

Leaver, R. A. *A Short History of Saint Mary's Chapel Castle Street Reading,* 1973

Lloyd, Frances *Woodley in the Nineteenth Century,* 1990

Lovett, R. History of the London Missionary Society, 1899

Man, J. *The Stranger in Reading,* 1810

Marsh, Catherine. *Life of the Rev. William Marsh DD by his daughter,* 1867

Neill, S. *A History of Christian Missions,* 1964

North, L. *Royal Reading's Colourful Past,* 1979

Payne, E. A. *The Baptists of Berkshire,* 1951

Pevsner, N. and Sherwood, Jennifer. *The Buildings of England, Oxfordshire,* 1974

Phillips, Daphne *The Story of Reading,* 1980

Reynolds, J. S. *The Evangelicals at Oxford 1735-1871,* 1953
   Canon Christopher of St Aldates Oxford, 1967

Smyth, C. *Simeon and Church Order,* 1937

Southerton, P. *The Story of a Prison,* 1975

Stock, E. *History of the Church Missionary Society,* 1899-1916
Summers, W. H. *County Congregational History,* 1905
Summerson, J. *Georgian London,* 1962
Wesley, J. *Journals*
Talbot, W. *Narrative of the Whole of His Proceedings relative to Jonathan Britain,* 1772
Young, Elizabeth & W. *London's Churches,* 1986

In addition, the *Dictionary of National Biography, Who was Who* and past issues of the *Reading Mercury, Berkshire* and *Reading Chronicles,* the *Oxford Diocesan Year Book* and *Crockford's Clerical Directory* have been consulted. The chief primary sources have been the considerable archive material held by the Chapel itself, including minutes, account-books, old magazines etc and material accumulated by Rev Robin Leaver, together with the Minute Book dated 1836-95 which is held in the Berkshire Record Office at Shire Hall. Copies of most of the Berkshire-related volumes cited above are located in the County Local Studies Collection at the County Reference Library, Reading.

NOTES

i   As Bishop of Ely, James Yorke ordained Charles Simeon.

ii   According to Cecil; an unnamed biographer in the *Evangelical Magazine* gives Caversham Park as Cadogan's birthplace.

iii J. S. Reynolds in *The Evangelicals at Oxford,* suggests that Edward Spencer (1740-1819), later Rector of Winkfield, Wilts, may have been the victim.

iv   The arrival in England of the Elgin Marbles in 1803 influenced the 'Greek Revival' in architecture, of which the façade of St Mary's Castle Street is a late example.

v   The correspondent's figures do not exactly agree with the Chapel accounts which show the collection as £119 less and the subscription as £1550.

vi   Probably John Russell (1745-1806), well-known for his portraits of the Royal Family and celebrities of the day. His son, Wiliam (1780-1870) was a more contemporary academician though rather less of a household name.

vii Sherman preached in the morning only. In the evening, the preacher was Andrew Reed (1787-1862), Minister of Wycliffe Chapel, London.

viii For further information on Bell's hymnody, see the author's pamphlet, *The Hymn-Writers of Reading.*

ix   Sonia Cole in her biography of the anthropologist, Louis Leakey, *Leakey's Luck,* identifies Col Bazett as his grandfather. Consterdine, however, writing nearer to events, states clearly that it was his brother, Mr R. Y. Bazett, who was father to Mary Bazett, Leakey's mother, and her sisters. This conclusion is corroborated by examination of the census of 1881 and local directories.

x   Although E. R. Hewett held the incumbency for eleven years, his ministry effectively ceased after nine.

APPENDICES

APPENDIX ONE: SHORT BIOGRAPHIES OF THE MINISTERS OF ST MARY'S, CASTLE STREET AND THEIR ASSISTANTS

A   MINISTERS/INCUMBENTS

1798-1800 Wiliam Green M, CHC. Resigned through ill-health, died shortly after.

1802-1805 Mr Bickerdike. An obscure figure.

1805-1807 Henry Gauntlett (1761-1833). Ordained 1786. C, Tilshead & Imber, Wilts 1800, Botley, Hants 1804, Wellington, Shropshire 1807, Nettlebed and Pishill, Oxon 1811. Olney, Bucks (1815, V). Pub: 1807 *Selection of Psalms and Hymns;* 1810 *Letters to the Stranger in Reading;* 1821 *Exposition of the Book of Revelation;* 1835 *Sermons.*

1807-1821 No regular minister.

1821-1836 James Sherman (1796-1862). Cheshunt College. Ordained, CHC, 1818. M, Bath and Bristol. 1836 M, Surrey Chapel, Blackfriars. 1854 Blackheath. Pub: 1826 *A Guide to Acquaintance with God,* 1830 *The Remembrance of Christ's Love;* 1841 *Hymns for the Use of Surrey Chapel;* 1848 *The Pastor's Wife;* 1850 *William Allen, A lecture.*

1836-1852 Charles James Goodhart (1804-92). Trinity Coll. Cambridge. D, 1827, P, 1828. C, Haselbury-Bryan, Dorset. 1831, Broad Chalke, Wilts 1852. I, Park Chapel, Chelsea. (1853-68, S, London Society for the Promotion of Christianity among the Jews — SPCJ). 1868. R, Wetherden, Haughley, Suffolk. Pub *The Light of Prophecy.*

1852-1888. George Ibberson Tubbs (1812-93). Highbury College Ordained, Congregational ministry, 1838. M, Independent Chapel, Warminster. D, 1847, P, 1848. 1851. C, Holy Trinity, Newington, Surrey. 1867. Ch, New Union Workhouse, Reading.

1888-1895 Hubert Brooke. St John's, Cambridge. D, 1875, P, 1876. C, SS Andrew and Mary Magdalene, Maidenhead. 1877. St Bride, Liverpool (1878-85, PC). 1885-7. Resident, Great Malvern. 1895. Winter Ch, Les Avants, Switzerland. 1897. I, St Margaret, Brighton. 1910-16. CMS Commissioner. Died 1930. Pub: 1888 *The Vision of the Candlestick* 1890 *The Temple of His Body;* 1897 *Personal Consecration;* 1905 *The Great High Priest* 1911 *The Fact and Features of the Lord's Return.*

1895-1915 James Consterdine (1852-1925). Lincoln Coll, Oxford. 1876. C, Christ Church, Westminster. 1883, Ch, Peshawar. 1885. I, St John, Ashbourne, Derbyshire. 1887. S, SE District, CPAS. 1891. C, Little Heath, Herts (1894, V). 1915. R, Edgware. Pub: 1902 *The Early History of St Mary's, Castle Street.*

1915-1919 Clifton David Frank Waters. Cambridge. D, 1906, P, 1907. C, St John, Upper Holloway. 1907. Walthamstow East. 1910. St Andrew, Watford. 1919. V, Mattersey, Notts. 1925-53. R, Clayworth, Notts.

1919-1922 Frank Burnett. Born 1874. Nonconformist M. D, 1914, P, 1915. C, St Mary the Virgin., Colchester. 1922. C, St Anne, Stamford Hill and Ch, Prince of Wales Hospital, Tottenham. 1925-42. R, Stoke St Michael, Coventry.

1923-1928 Sydney Robert Skeens (1871-1943). D, 1898, P, 1899. Served with CMS, Uganda to 1920. BA Durham, 1910. 1916-20 RD, Singo and Buwekula. 1922. C, Northwood.

1928-35 V. Yatesbury, Wilts. Later lived in Bournemouth.

1928-39 Edwin Robert Hewitt. St Aidan's, Birkenhead. D, 1918, P, 1920. C, St Nicholas, Colchester. 1923. St Paul, Northumberland Heath, Erith. 1924. SMCS. Died 1963.

1939-1946 Sidney William Saker. Born 1908. U. Durham, LC Divinity. D, 1935, P, 1936. C, St Andrew, Islington. 1938. Bermondsey. 1946. Midlands Organising S, BCMS. 1953. SW Area S, SAMS. Living in Leicester.

1947-1950 Oswald Canning Goold. Trinity Coll, Dublin. D, 1915, P, 1916. C, St John's, Carlisle. 1917. St Thomas, Crookes, Sheffield. 1924. V, Emmanuel, Sheffield. 1928. St Simon and St Jude, Southport. 1933. Deputation S, Sudan United Mission. 1940-1. R, Little Leighs, Essex. 1942. Chaplain, RAFVR. 1945. V, St Matthew, West Ham. 1951. Deputation S, Irish Church Missions. 1953. Sudan United Mission.

1951-1952 Michael Willoughby Dewar. Born 1921. Emmanuel, Cambridge. St Aidans, Birkenhead. D, 1949, P, 1950. C, Shankill, Lurgan, Co. Armagh. 1952. Ballymacarrett. 1955. R, Scarva. 1960. Ch, Harcourt School, Andover. 1964, C-i-c, Magherally with Annaclone. 1973-86. I, Helen's Bay. Currently resident in Cheltenham.

1953-1961 Harold Peacock (1905-88). London College of Divinity. D, 1940, P, 1941. C, St John, Parkstone, Dorset. 1943. V, Hennock, Newton Abbot.

1961-1963 Frederick Thomas Ellis. D, 1945, P, 1946. C, Christ Church, Beckenham. 1948. V, St Peter, Tunbridge Wells. 1951. St Cuthbert, West Hampstead.

1964-1965. Bryan Edwin Hardman. Moore Th Coll, Sydney. London Bible Coll. Selwyn, Cambridge (PhD). 1955-7 and 1957-60 C, Hurstville, Sydney, 1957. Summer Hill, Sydney. 1964-5. Ed, *English Churchman.* 1965. V, St Andrew the Less, Cambridge. 1968. Vice-Pr, Adelaide Bible Institute.

1965-1968 Gordon Murray. Born 1933. St Cath, Cambridge. Clifton Th Coll. D, 1959, P, 1960. C, St James, Hereford. 1962. Uphill, Somerset. 1965-71. Ed, *English Churchman.* 1968-75. Pr, Kensit Bible Coll. 1976-8. Asst Master, Sandown, IOW. Later Baptist M, Felixstowe, Suffolk.

1968-1970 Dennis Parker. Born 1922. Tyndale Hall, Bristol. D, 1964, P, 1965. CX Polegate, Sussex. 1970—87. V, Newdigate, Surrey. Currently resident in Dorking.

1971-1977 Robin A. Leaver. Born 1939. Clifton TC, D, 1964, P, 1965. C, Gypsy Hill. 1967. Great Baddow. 1977-86. I, St Mary, Cogges, Witney, Oxon. Currently resident in USA. Pub: *A Short History of Saint Mary's Chapel, Castle Street, Reading; The Doctrine of Justification in the Church of England; Music as Preaching.*

1978-1984 Cyril Theodore Martin Browne. Born 1912. Bible Churchmen's Coll, Bristol. D, 1935, P, 1936. C, Emmanuel, Holloway. 1938. Christ Church, Finchley. 1941. Broadwater, Worthing. 1943. PC, St Matthew, Muswell Hill. 1950. V,

St John Clerkenwell. 1962. Greenwich. 1974. R, Tilston & V, Shocklach, Cheshire. 1985-8. LO, Southam, Wks. Currently resident, Tunbridge Wells.

1984-1990 Allan Harold Leslie Bowhill. Born 1943. Trinity, Bristol. D, 1982, P, 1983. C, St Luke, Wolverhampton. 1990. R, Keinton Mandeville and Lydford on Fosse, Somerset. (1991, also Barton St David and Kingweston.)

1991- David Norman Samuel. Born 1930. U. Wales. Edinburgh Th Coll. U. Hull (PhD 1983). Baptist M. D, 1961, P, 1962. C, Bishops Stortford. 1965. Bedford. 1968. I, Ashby with Fensby and Brigsley; Beelsby; East and West Ravendale with Hatcliffe, Lincs. 1983. Dr, Church Society. Pub: 1979 *The Evangelical Succession* (Ed); 1982 *Pope or Gospel*.

B. CURATES AND OTHERS

1808-1837 Joseph Watkins. Ordained 1808. Died 1837.

1842-1843 Edward Haskins. C, Exbury, Fawley, Hants in 1850.

1845-1846 Charles Dent Bell (1818-98). Trinity, Dublin. D, 1843, P, 1844. C, Hampton-in Arden. 1846. St Mary-in-the-Castle, Hastings. 1854. I, St John's, Hampstead. 1861. V, Ambleside (1872, with Rydal). 1872. R, St Mary, Cheltenham. Pub: 1861 *Night Scenes from the Bible;* 1873 *The Saintly Calling;* 1882 *Hymns for Church and Chamber; Life of Henry Martyn; Commentary on Hebrews XI.*

1846-52 Charles Hole. Trinity, Cambridge. D, 1846, P, 1847. 1852. Chaplain, Reading Union, 1858. C, Shanklin, IOW, 1868-76. R, Loxbeare, Devon. 1879. L, Ecclesiastical History, King's College, London. Also Ch to Lord Sackville. Pub 1865 *Brief Biographical Dictionary,* 1871-3 *Life of the Revd. and Ven. William Whitworth Phelps;* 1887 *Manual of the Book of Common Prayer;* 1896 *Early History of the CMS.*

c. 1855 C. Stirling. D, 1851, P, 1852. 1867-92. V, New Malden with Coombe, Surrey.

1864-1866 Robert Towers. St Bees. D, 1858, P, 1859, C, Bromfield, Cheshire. 1861, Hexham, Northumberland. 1862. Islington. 1866. Hastings. 1867-9, PC, St Paul, Kilburn. 1870-1914. V, St Andrew and St Philip, N Kensington.

1867-1878 C. Gordon Smythe. D, 1863, P, 1864. Later C, St Paul, Macclesfield. 1883. R, Bright, Downpatrick.

1878-1879 Sydenham Lynes Dixon. KC, London. D, 1876, P, 1877. C, Greyfriars, Reading. 1879, V, St John the Evangelist, King's Lynn. 1884. St George, Worthing. 1888. M, Park Chapel, Chelsea. 1898-1905. V, St John, Lowestoft. 1905. St Peter, Paddington. 1915. Sandown, IOW. 1924, PC, St George, Brighton. Died 1932.

1879-1882 James Hussey. Wadham Coll, Oxford. D, 1874, P, 1875. C, St James, Poole. 1876. Compton Chamberlayne, Wilts. 1882. Durweston with Bryanston, Dorset. 1886-1906. R, Pimperne nr Blandford, Dorset.

1882-1883 Charles Duppuy. Ordained D, 1876, P, 1877.

1883-1887 Sholto John Henry Newman. Queens Coll, Cambridge. D, 1879, P, 1880. 1879. C, Holy Trinity, Tulse Hill. 1881. Davenham, Cheshire. 1887-1930. V, Emmanuel, Hastings.

1887-1889 Robert Thompson. St Aidan's, Birkenhead. D, 1885, P, 1886. C, St Luke, Nottingham. 1890. Bryanston and Durweston, Dorset. 1893. Faringdon, Berks. 1895. V, Longcot with Fernham, Berks. 1902. Holy Trinity, West Bromwich. 1916. Emmanuel, Market Drayton. 1928-32. R, Eastrop, Hants.

1889 1893 Athur Swinton Weatherhead. Kings Coll, Cambridge. D, 1889, P, 1890. 1893. C, Stoke next Guildford. 1896. Tonbridge. 1899. V, St James, Hereford. 1910. Hoily Trinity, Huddersfield. 1923. R, Trowbridge. 1929. C, St Mary in the Marsh, Norwich. 1930-38. R, Beeston, St Andrew, Norwich.

1893-1895 Harrington Clare Lees (1871-1929). St John's Coll/Ridley Hall, Cambridge. D, 1893, P, 1894. 1895. Anglican Ch, Turin. 1897. C, Childwall, Liverpool. 1900. V, St John, Kenilworth 1907-19. Christchurch, Beckenham. 1908-19. Diocesan Mission Preacher, Rochester. 1919. V, Swansea. 1921. Abp of Melbourne. Pub: 1910 *The King's Coming;* 1916 *The Practice of the Presence of Christ;* 1917 *St Paul's Friends;* 1919 *God's Garden and Ours.*

1896-1897 Edward Mansel Townshend. Kings Coll, London/Clare Coll/Ridley Hall, Cambridge. D, 1886, P, 1889. C, Holy Trinity, Tewkesbury. 1888. Anglican Ch, Avranches, Normandy. 1889. Ch, Dr Barnardo's Homes. 1892. C, Christ Church, Spitalfields. 1892. Waltham Abbey. 1894-5. Christ Church, Harrogate. 1897, Holy Trinjity, Sydenham. 1898-1947. R, Llanvapley, Abergavenny.

1898-1900 Percy George Wood (1861-1938). LCD. D, 1885, P, 1886. C, St Paul, Brixton. 1887. South Heysham, Norfolk. 1892. CMS, Cairo. 1900. Organising S, CMS, Lichfield and Hereford. 1910. C, St Michael, Stonebridge. 1915. St Philip, Norbury. 1916. Immanuel, Streatham. 1926. St Stephen, S Lambeth. Retired 1929.

1902 1903 Augustus Hyde Treadway Clarke. Kings Coll, Cambridge. D, 1902, P, 1905. 1904. C, St Matthias, Tulse Hill. 1907. Hammersmith. 1909. Christ Church, Woburn Square. 1910. Christ Church, Albany St. 1912. St Martin with St Paul, Canterbury. 1915. R, St John and St Mary, Devizes, Wilts. 1937-46. PC, St Katherine, Savernake Forest, Wilts.

1903-1904 John Goodenough Bayly Hollins (1858−1931) Hertford C, Oxford, Ordained, 1885. 1894. CMS. 1905-9. C, St Andrew & Mary Magdalene, Maidenhead. 1909-22. V, Heywood, Salisbury.

1904-1910 Charles Horace Bellamy (d. 1954). Wycliffe Hall, Oxford. D, 1904, P, 1905. 1911. C, Holy Trinity, Tunbridge Wells. 1919. V, St Simon, Hammersmith. 1930-54. St Mary's, Longfleet, Poole.

1911-1912 Francis Rowling (1866-1949). C. M. Coll, Islington. D, 1893, P, 1895 (in Africa). BA (Durham) 1906. Served with CMS in Uganda to 1921. 1923. R, Harlton, Ely. 1927-34. Seaborough, Devon. 1917. Pub: 1912 *Guide to Luganda Prose Composition;* 1927/29 *Simple Science for African Schools;* 1930 *The Parables for Africans;* 1933/8. *The Miracles of Jesus.*

1913-1915 Cecil Arthur James Beatty. Wycliffe, Oxford. Ex-solicitor. D, 1908, P, 1910. 1908-12. C, Coombe Down, Bath. 1915. Duffield, Derby. 1917, St Mary, Leamington. 1921. St James, Clapham Park. 1926. St James, West Streatham. 1927. R, Milston with Brigmurston, Wilts.

1924-1928 Edwin Robert Hewett — see above.

1933-1935 Arthur Baker (1856-1935). U. Durham. D, 1883, P, 1884. 1902-10. V, St Katharine, Savernake Forest 1910-19. St Thomas, N Kensington. 1919-26. Littledean, Gloucs.

1937 and 1939 Samuel Victor Floyd Griffiths. Queens/Ridley Hall, Cambridge D, 1910, P, 1912. Eight curacies including

Broadwater, Worthing, 1922-4. 1936-56. LO, St Mark's, Tollington Park. 1945. Ch, St Pancras Cemetery.

1937 Nicholas Albert Edward Earle. U. Manchester. Exeter/Wycliffe Hall, Oxford. D, 1915, P, 1916. 1927-32. V, St John's, Birkdale, Pub: 1933 *The Coming Kingdom and the Coming King.*

1938-1939 Robert Wakefield Benson. Exeter/Wycliffe Hall, Oxford. D, 1925, P, 1926. Curate, Holy Trinity, Worthing. 1929. P-i-c, St Cuthbert, Hoddesdon. 1930-36. V, St Barnabas, York. 1939-48. V, Weald, Kent.

1950-1953 Frederick Augustus Watney. Born 1879. LCD. D, 1902, P, 1903. C, St Thomas, Lambeth. 1909. Organising S, SPCJ (1915-18). Deputation S. 1919. V, All Saints, Camberwell. 1929. R, Knoishall with Buxlow. 1934. C, (to C Bellamy), St Mary, Longfleet. 1936-9. V, St Cuthbert, Hampstead. Died 197? Pub 1917 *God's Key to World Blessing.*

1952-1953. Edmund George Arnold Dunn. LC Divinity. D. 1900, P, 1901. 1938-51. Ch, Whiteley Village, Walton on Thames.

1977-1978 John Harbury Hill (1909-80). Bristol. Formerly served C of E in S Africa. D & P, 1964. LO Oxford from 1970.

Key: Abp. Archbishop; C. Curate; Ch. Chaplain; CHC. Countess of Huntingdon's Connexion; C-i-c. Curate-in-charge; D. Deacon; Dr. Director; Ed. Editor; I. Incumbent; L. Lecturer; LCD. London College of Divinity; LO. Licensed to officiate; M. Minister; P. Priest; PC. Perpetual Curate; P-i-c. Priest-in-charge; Pr. Principal; R. Rector; RD. Rural Dean; S. Secretary; V. Vicar.

APPENDIX TWO: OVERSEAS MISSIONAIRES ASSOCIATED WITH ST MARY'S, CASTLE STREET

1834 John Ross. LMS. Co-worker of Sherman, went out to Berbice, Br. Guyana. Invalided home. Later served as pastor of a church in Woodbridge, Suffolk.

1836 Rev. Mr Loveless. Received gratuity of £2 from the Trustees. Described as missionary in India for 18 years. Otherwise connection with SMCS unknown.

1850 Thomas Valpy French (1825-1891). CMS. See Chapters IV and XI.

1883 James Consterdine (1852-1925) See Chapter XII. Consterdine's brother, Reginald Henry Consterdine (1863-1938), was a CMS Missionary in Japan 1893-1900, and his son, Rudolph, worked for the YMCA in Cairo for many years, later coming to live at Padworth. Both preached at SMCS on occasions.

1888 Edward Mansel Townshend, Anglican Ch., Avranches, Normandy, 1888/9. See App 1.

1891 Thomas Simmonds, CEYMCA. Member of Men's Bible Class run by one of the Bazetts. Left 31/10/91 for China and served in Szechuen Province. Returned 1906.

1891 James Harris Redman (1849-92). CMS. From Purton, Wilts. Had been Secretary of YMCA, Reading. See Chapter XI. Redman's brothers, John and Alfred Ernest, were also CMS missionaries in what is now Pakistan.

1892 The Misses Whitby. One called Mary, one became Mrs Pugh; previously in charge of the YWCA in Reading, but otherwise personal details scarce. Went out together to Maritzburg in Natal 21/4/92 to work among the Zulus. Mary suffered severe attack of fever soon after arrival.

1892 Louisa, Mary and Sibella Bazett (CMS); Rev. Harry Leakey; Rev George Burns. See Chapters XI and XII.

1892 Rev Percy George Wood (1861-1938), Served as a CMS Missionary in Old Cairo 1892-7, resigning on health grounds. Later Organising Secretary for CMS in the Lichfield and Hereford dioceses 1900-10.

1893 Rev (later Canon) Frank Rowling (1866-1949). CMS. Engineer from Leeds. Worked in Entebbe. On loan to Conference of British Missionary Societies Literature Committee 1921-3. Retired 1923. Translated St John's Gospel into Lusoga.

1894 Mr and Mrs Richard J Hunt (SAMS). See Chapter XI.

1894 Rev Thomas Davis, from Abergavenny, went out to Bombay October 1894, aged 26, to work among Moslems, resigning 1906.

1894 Miss Anna Maria Baker, aged 22, Assistant Secretary of the YWCA in Reading, went to Hong Kong as FES missionary. On dissolution of FES transferred to CMS South China Mission, 1899. Resigned, 1909, prior to marriage to Mr C. E. Thompson.

1894 Rev John Goodenough Baly Hollins (1858-1931), CMS, of Ramsgate served in Palestine and Egypt 1894-1902, resigned on medical grounds.

1895 Rev Hubert Brooke. See Chapter XI.

1895 Rt Rev Harrington Clare Lees (1871-1929). Accepted by CMS with a view to theological college work with "native candidates" but suffered breakdown in health. See Chapter XI.

1896 Florence Mary Sells (1869-1856) from Redhill, trained as nurse at Royal Berkshire Hospital. Went out to Old Cairo as CMS missionary, retiring 1930. Latterly lived in her native Redhill.

1896 Miss Minnie Alice Wood, born in Ceylon, where her father, Rev D Wood served 1867-93. As governess aged 25, went out to the Ceylon Mission, Kandy. Resigned 1898 on medical grounds.

1896 Miss V. Von Himpe M.D., CEZMS, served in Calcutta, India, in charge of hospital.

1897 Deaconess Gertrude Ellen Withers, CMS, 25-year old teacher of callisthenics before going out to India. Married 1898 Rev A Outram (1872-1937), who had gone out to India the same year. Outram resigned on medical grounds 1905 when the couple returned to England.

1897 Matilda Phoebe Silman, worshipped at SMCS while working in Reading as Board School Teacher, married Rev T. J. Dennis (1869-1917), returning with him to Niger the same year. Dennis, from Eastbourne, served in CMS Niger Mission from 1893, became Archdeacon of Upper Niger, 1905. He died in 1917 when *SS Karina*, on which he was returning to England, was torpedoed. Mrs Dennis survived him forty years, living latterly in Parkstone, Dorset.

1897 Helen Wood (1873-1928), CMS, sister of Minnie Wood, left for China, serving initially in Chekiang Mission, Taichow. Married 1903 Thomas Gaunt (1875-1962). Gaunt came out 1899 and was Principal, Anglo-Chinese School, Hangchow. Later ordained (deadon 1907), retired 1939. Their son, J. A. Gaunt, also CMS missionary from 1929.

1898 Ven. Ernest Scudamore Tanner CMS. See Chapter Xi.

1898 Sydney Robert Skeens (1871-1943), CMS, served Uganda 1898-1920, mainly at Iganga. Married 1907 Sophie Rose Tanner (1865-1950), from Aldershot, who had gone out to Africa in 1899.

1898 W. H. Newell Accepted for training 1895, went out to Peru 1898, died 1902.

1899 Mabel Gertrude Bazett; Richard Herbert Leakey. See Chapter XI.

1899 Edith Catherine Pike (1871-1944), CMS, accompanied Rev and Mrs R. H. Leakey to Uganda June 1899. Nurse from Co. Down. Served mainly at Kaberole in Toro region. Retired 1925 but subsequently reaccepted, serving 1935-9.

1899 Mr and Mrs W. B. Milsum joined China Inland Mission 1899. No other details known.

1900 Rev George Thomas Basden went out to Ouitsha on the Niger. Preached at SMCS and was commended in prayer 2/9/1900, sailing 8/9. Understood to have been CMS missionary but not traced in CMS records. Later Archdeacon.

1900 Miss Helen Jane Dewe (1874-1957), CMS, commended at Prayer Meeting 23/9/99 before sailing to Palestine to undertake educational work on Mount of Olives. Married 1905 Alfred Elias Mitchell, schoolmaster. Mitchell served CMS in Sierra Leone from 1902, joined Palestine Mission 1904. Later worked in Persia but resigned from CMS in 1919 following ordination to become a missionary of SPCJ.

1907 Rev John Britton went out to Uganda. Married 1914 Annie Young Harvey who died shortly after their return to Uganda.

1910 Mr Arthur Minchin (1881-1973). See Chapter XII. Went out to North-West Canada as missionary. Subsequently ordained.

1935 Mr Charles Richmond, BCMS, served in Kenya to 1940. Later ordained and ministered in the USA until death in 1988; his brother, Denis, is a life-long member of SMCS.

196- Mr and Mrs Ian Bevington, OMF. Rachel Peacock, daughter of Rev. Harold Peacock, called to mission field after working as nurse at Mildmay Mission Hospital, London; with husband, Ian, has served with OMF in Thailand over 20 years. He is involved in teaching and evangelistic work.

1976 Rev Richard and Wendy Sutton CMS, served in the Sindh region of Pakistan to 1979. Wendy previously served briefly with Ruanda Mission. Richard's mission included agricultural development work. Currently Vicar, Christ Church, Sidcup. See also Chapter XVI.

1978 Miss Iris Dodd (1935-83). See Chapter XVII.

1985 Mark and Isobel Jones worshipped occasionally at St Mary's Castle Street before going out to Kenya as short-term missionary-teachers. See Chapter XVII. Mark is now Curate to former BCMS missionary, Rev Edward Malcolm, at St Luke's Wolverhampton.

SMCS-connected missionaries have served in the following countries/territories: Argentina, Australia, Canada, China, Egypt, Guyana, Hong Kong, India, Italy, Kenya, Muscat, Natal, Nigeria, Pakistan, Palestine, Paraguay, Romania, Tanganyika, Thailand, Uganda.

The chapel has also supported a number of missionaries under the Ruanda/MAM and BCMS partnership schemes. Currently these are Andrew and Felicity Maclay in Burundi and Ian and Val MacFarlane in Ethiopia.

APPENDIX THREE: THE TRUSTEES OF ST MARY'S, CASTLE STREET
Listed according to date of appointment.

1797 Peter William French, chemist and druggist, opposed episcopacy, res 1838: Thomas Ring (1761-1840), surgeon, Warden and Treasurer 1838-40: Jonathan Tanner, brewer, deceased by 1836, 1st Lieutenant of Reading Volunteers and Treasurer of Bible Society locally: Thomas Tanner, linen and woollen draper, later resided in Bath but occasionally attended meetings: James May, yeoman, of Englefield: Joseph Baylis (1745-1823), clerk of St Giles' Church; Joseph Young, bacon-merchant, Treasurer 1797-1838; Thomas Willatts, opposed episcopacy, res 1838; Robert Lawrance, draper, Warden, d1838; Richard Harbert, lived away from Reading latterly, but attended important meetings in 1836 and 1838.

Pre-1836. Thomas Stratton, retired bookseller, d1837; Alfred Compeigne, attorney, d1837; Richard Billing (1785-1853) architect and builder, Chapel Warden and also Treasurer of the Trustees from 1840, Mayor of Reading, 1852, res Trusteeship, 1852; Charles May, chemist and druggist, signatory of 1856 Trust Deed; James Trendell, gentleman, also believed to be silversmith, signatory of 1856 Trust Deed, Warden 1852; James Bourne, opposed episcopacy, dismissed from office 1838 after joining 'another society'; Thomas Skeate Workman, surgeon, Warden and Joint-Treasurer 1840, d1851.

1838 Charles Cowan, doctor of medicine. Signatory of 1856 Trust Deed; Thomas Haggard; Thomas Lawrance, draper, Burgess of Reading Corporation and Mayor in 1834, later resident in Gloucestershire, signatory of 1856 Trust Deed; Mr Owen and Mr Heathcock, rarely attended meetings; Thomas Lodge, gentleman, later resident in Croydon, signatory of 1856 Deed.

1849 Henry Chase, solicitor, named in 1856 Trust Deed as Rev Henry John Neale Chase, clerk, of Bridge, near Canterbury, Kent, having taken deacon's orders in 1855, though not priested until 1866, PC of St Mary's, Hatfield in 1883, res Trusteeship in 1893 aged 80, while living at Tunbridge Wells.

1851 John Woodroffe Workman, surgeon, elected in succession to his brother, T. S. Workman, signatory of 1856 Trust Deed, d1894.

1855 Thomas Hawkins, brewer, d1893; Robert Hewett (1811-1904), brewer; James Lodge, gentleman; Robert Parsons Miller (1818-1905), chemist and druggist; Martin Hope Sutton (1815-1901), seedsman; Joseph Whatley, gentleman.

1856 Also named in the 1856 Deed, Henry Hibberd, farmer, possibly appointed in place of C. Simonds (who was proposed in 1855 but apparently declined) living in Dartford in 1888, but could not be traced in 1893.

1873 Daniel Heelas, draper, d1910; George Philbrick, tanner, Warden, d1922; William Butler Young; Charles Holbrook, res 1894.

1893 James Dymore Brown, brewer, res 1902; Lt-Col Richard Bazett (1840-1912); Thomas Edward Hewett (1850-1933), son of Robert Hewett, later Chmn of Reading Gas Co; John Hill, India rubber merchant, res 1910; Lieut-Gen Duncan John McGregor, d1909; Arthur Warwick Sutton, d1925.

1894 Major Edward Phillips, d1915; Colonel Robert Frederick Williams, formerly stationed in Bombay, d1906; John Warrick, son of bargee, manufacturer of delivery bicycles and ice-cream tricycles, res 1922, d1925.

1905 Lieut-Col Henry Ronald Buchanan-Dunlop, Royal Artillery, d1941; Charles Woide Goodhart, gentleman, d1914; Rev Daniel Bell Hankin, formerly (from 1877) V of St Jude's Mildmay Park, now resident in Reading, res 1910, d1914; Joseph Charles Falla, Chapel Clerk, d1906.

1910 Ernest Sutton, res 1919; Edwin Hewett, son of Thomas Hewett, Minister 1928-39, d1963; Rev Hubert Brooke, former Minister of the Chapel, resident in Hindhead and Bournemouth during Trusteeship, d1930; Rev (later Rt Rev) Harrington Clare Lees, (1871-1929) former curate, res 1921; Augustus Walter Cruikshank, d1918; William George Newbery, pawnbroker, res 1920, reappointed 1927, d1930 Rev (later Canon)Sydenham Dixon, former curate, d1932.

1927 Allan Ernest McAdam, solicitor, of Blackheath, d1930. Miss Jessie Flanagan (1873-1955), Warden); Miss Catherine Hart (1865-1936), daughter of John Hart, Ironmonger; Arthur Charles Harding (1887-1947), Insurance Agent, Warden; Percy King Allen, architect, resident in Tunbridge Wells, d1944; Rev Walter Joseph Latham, V of Immanuel, Streatham Common, 1914-26, Public Preacher, Dio. Southwark 1928-36.

1932 Rev Herbert William Hinde (later Prebendary), Prin of Oak Hill Theological College 1932-45, res 1947; Rev George Thomas Manley, V of St Luke's, Hampstead 1930-40, res 1947; Rev Earle Legh Langston, R of Sevenoaks, 1929-37, res 1951, later officiated in Dio of Uganda; Rev Alfred St John Thorpe (1885-197?), V Christ Church, Beckenham, 1923-35, Walford, 1936-57, res 1950; Rev Charles Horace Bellamy, former curate, d1954; Rev Hugh Baird Richardson, Irish Church Missions 1926-33, R of Kingham 1933-50, later lived in Worthing, d1966; Frederick William Carter, of Redhill, Surrey, later of Eastbourne, res 1957; Isabel Mary Hewett, sister of Edwin Hewett, d1971.

1948 Rev Douglas Horsefield (1893-1972) R of Newton Purcell with Shelswell, nr Buckingham 1947-54, lived in St Leonards after retirement; Rev Arthur William Handley Moule, R of Woolhampton 1943-64, later lived in Mabledon, Kent, Chmn of Trustees 1963-8, d1972; Dr Joseph Tinsley, Lecturer at Reading University, Warden, later Professor of Soil Science, Aberdeen. res 1987; Miss Edith Frankum (1879-1968), Matron of Battle Hospital, Warden.

1955 Rev (later Rt Rev) Russell Berridge White (1896-1978), Bp of Tonbridge 1959-68, Chairman, Trustees 1968-74; Rev (later Rt Rev) Gordon Savage (1915-90), Bp of Buckingham 1960-64 and Southwell 1964-70, res 1971; Rev Frederick Augustus Watney (1879-197?), res 1968; Rev Peter Cottingham, born 1924, V of St Clement's, Oxford, later held livings in South Mimms, Herts, 1968-81, Derby 1981-89, res 1989; Malcolm Henry MacQueen, Asst Sec, CPAS, res 1970.

1956 Audley F. Sutton, Chmn of Trustees (1957-63), d1963.

1964 Ernest William Appleby (1899-1984), Warden, Sec to Trustees since 1957, res 1981; Rev John Stewart Reynolds, born 1919, R of Besselsleigh with Dry Sandford, 1956-1985, now resident in Oxford, Chmn of Trustees, 1974-84*; Richard Sutton, born 1939, seedsman. Member of congregation, later ordained, res 1980; Rev John Beecroft Swinbank, Ch Bradfield College, Chmn of Local Trustees from 1965, d1989.

1968 Rev Richard Rayner, born 1924, held livings at Slough, York and Okehampton, Devon, res 1989; Gervase Duffield, publisher, of Appleford, near Didcot, res 1992; J Vellacott, farmer, res 1969.

1969 David Karsten, schoolteacher, member of congregation, now associated with ministry in Woodley *; Rev Anthony Grenville Pouncey, born 1911. V of St Peter's, Woking, 1967-79, later resident in Southsea, res 1979.

1973 Rev Roger Beckwith, born 1929, Warden of Latimer House, Oxford from 1973, Chmn of Trustees 1984-92, res Trusteeship 1992; Alan Green, Building Society Manager (retired), of Kennington, res 1980.

1974 Charles Borsley, born 1938, Treasurer of Trustees and Chapel Council, res on leaving congregation, 1991; Rev Tom Shaw, R of Drayton, Banbury, rarely attended, d1985.

1980 Rev C. Gordon F. Clark, born 1907, V of Crowborough 1948-67, now resident in Peterborough, res 1989; Rev John Frank Shearer, born 1935, R of Nuffield from 1967, Chmn of Trustees from 1992.*

1982 Mrs Barbara Hurst, daughter of Arthur Harding and wife of Rev J. Hurst, V of St Peter's, Tunbridge Wells, retired 1991, now resident in Poole.*

1983 Oliver Raymond Johnston (1927-85), Director of NFOL and Care Campaigns; Mark R. Clements, born 1954, Insurance Manager, Warden 1983-90.* (Mrs Jane Clements is present secretary to the Trustees).

1986 Hugh Craig, engineer, member of General Synod and lay reader, Bradfield.*

1989 Rev Fenn Robson, born 1930, Deputations Secretary of Irish Church Missions, 1982-6, resident in Abingdon *; Rev Dr David Samuel, born 1930, res 1990, Incumbent from 1991; David J. Dethridge, barrister. *.

1990 John B. Dearing, born 1946. Warden from 1985 *; Edward J. Malcolm, Warden from 1991 *.

*Present Trustees, February 1993.

INDEX

All figures in *italics* refer to illustrations

SUBSCRIBERS

Presentation Copies

1 The Trustees of St Mary's, Castle Street,
   Reading
2 The Diocese of Oxford
3 The Borough of Reading
4 Berkshire County Council, Archives
5 Berkshire County Library
6 Rev Dr David Samuel
7 William Appleby

8 John Dearing
9 Clive Birch
10 Rt Rev John Bone, Bishop of Reading
11 Rev C.T.M. Browne
12 Miss W.E. Mitchell
13 Mrs B. Over
14 Patrick J. Rose
15 Michael Dark
16 Peter J.R. Trout
17 Barbara Tiley
18 Vera Good
19 Leighton Yeo
21 Rev F. Robson
22
23 J.P. Westmacott
24 David Dethridge
25 Miss Penny Mark
26 R.T. Beckwith
27 Latimer House
28 C.G. Wootten
29 B.M. Hinton
30 G.Spriggs
31 Mrs D.J. Beddoes
32 M.S. & R. Gillett
33 G.W. Mill
34 Haydn Richards
35 Leslie Herbert Wicks
36 Rev C.G.F. Clark
37
38 Anne Gillibrand
39 Dennis Richmond
40 Michael J. Connelly
41 Canon Dr M.W. Dewar
42 H. Godwin Arnold
43 Mr & Mrs H.F. Andrews
44 Mrs H. Wilkins
45 Oak Hill College
46 Admiral Sir Anthony Griffin
47 Mark Clements
48 Trinity College Library, Bristol
49 Mark Jones
50 Ellen L. Halfacre
51 Malcolm Walker
52 Rev Allan Bowhill
53 A. Boult
54 Eileen Crombie
55 Charles Borsley
56 Dr A.G. Cumberland
57 Jonathan Fletcher

58 M. Megnauth
59 Dr R.E.B. Peake
60 Robert V. Masters
61 Philip Sizer
62 R.S. Aird
63 Chantrey Vellacott
64 Lambeth Palace Library
65 A.E. Watkins
66 Jonathan Everitt
67 D.A.P. Harvey
68 Mrs G. Naish
69 Reginald Meade
70 Mrs Elizabeth Sore
71 John Mason
72 Rev M.H. McGowan
73 R.J. Bolam
74 Mrs C. Richmond
75 R. Toop
76 Tony Hadland
77 G.P. Wild
78 Rev B. Dutson
79 Mrs Connie Sizer
80 Jane A. Welch
81 Earl and Gwen Williams
82 Lester Hines
83 Joseph Tinsley
84 Rev P.R. and Mrs M. Akehurst
85 Mrs E. O'Neill
86 Mr & Mrs H. Dallyn
87 Maria Petrovic
88 Peter Whyte
89 Rev John Shearer
90 Eddie Stock
91 Dorothy Barnes
92 The Borough Church of St Andrew &
   St Mary Magdalene, Maidenhead
93 George Reed
94 Bournemouth School
95 University of York
96 Roy Leonton
97 K. H. Rogers
98 Miss Julia Roe
99 Miss Laura Roe
100 Mr & Mrs D.B. Kimber
101 William & Grace Dearing
102 A.R. Goulder
103 Rev W.N. Elliott
104 Duncan Green
105 Mrs Maisie Legerton

St Mary's, Castle Street in Victorian times — the Church that would not die. (BLAT)

120